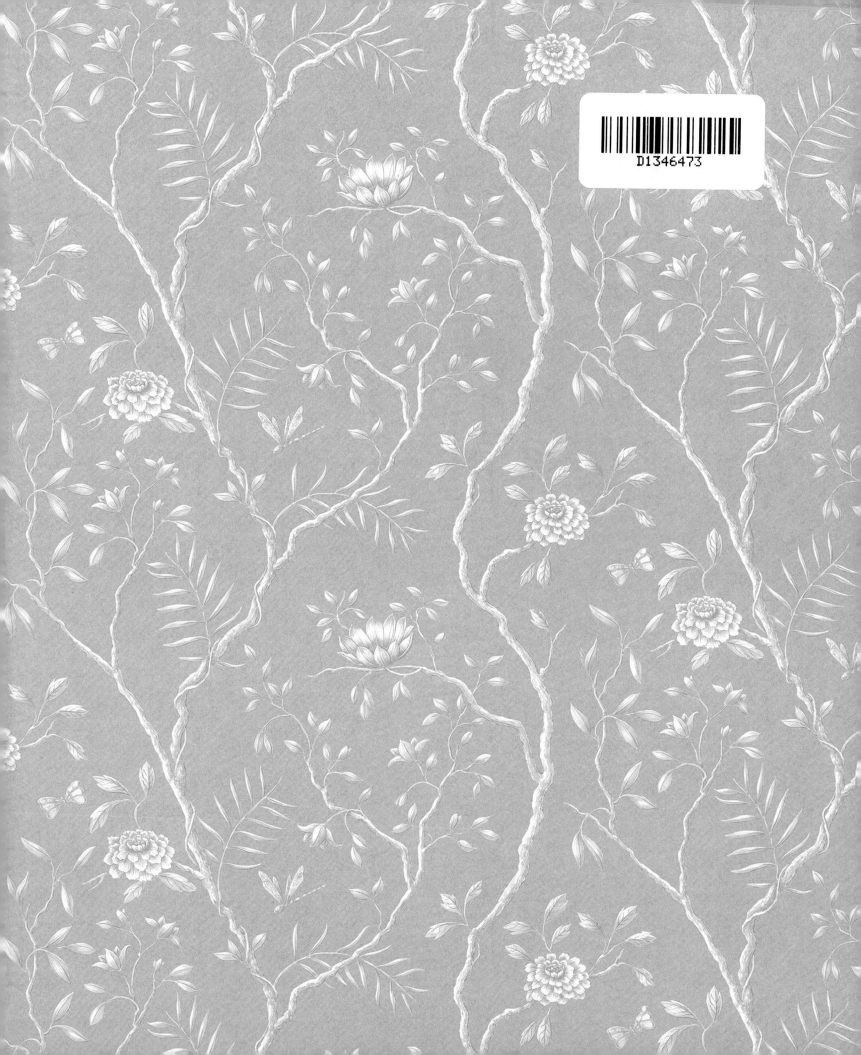

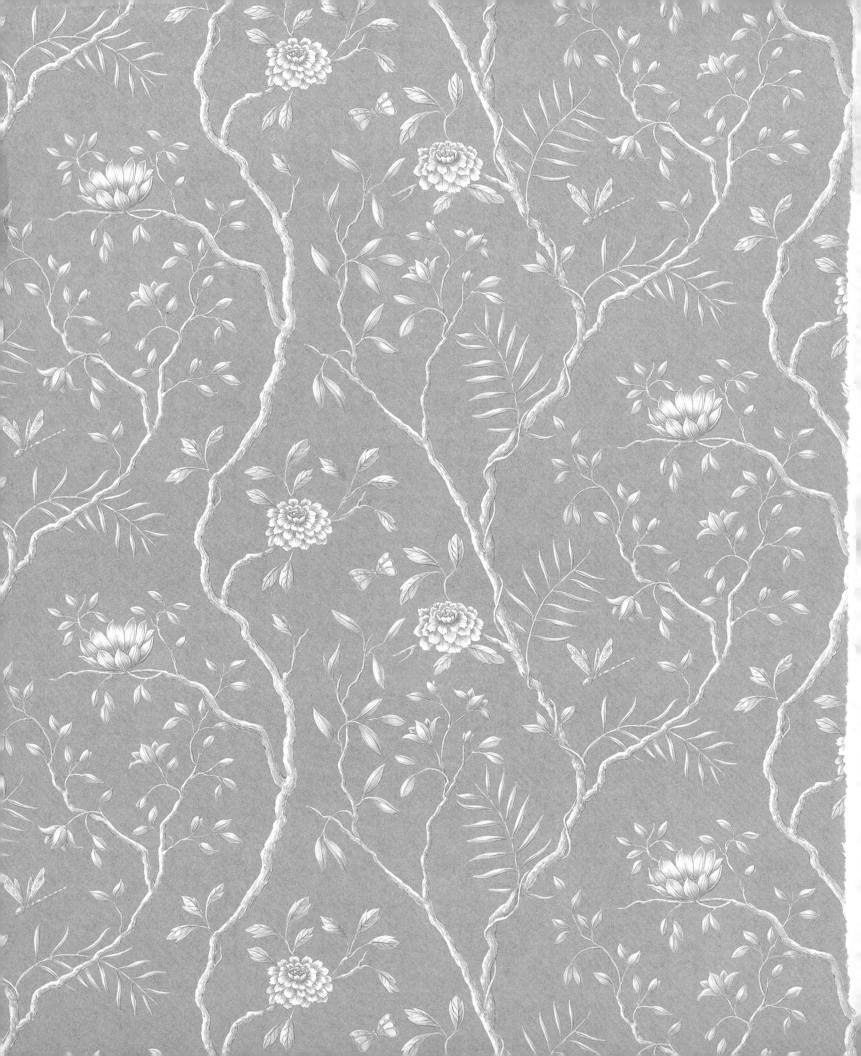

JOANNA WOOD

Dedicated to
Leonora & Harriet

JOANNA WOOD

INTERIORS FOR LIVING

By Joanna Wood with Sarah Edworthy

PRESTEL

Munich • London • New York

CONTENTS

FOREWORD
BY DAVID LINLEY

I met Joanna in 1982 when we were working on different parts of an interior design show house in Cornwall Terrace overlooking Regent's Park. Since then, we have collaborated on many projects varying in scale and style, from a bright yellow Rolls Royce to the opulent restoration of a 60,000 square foot heritage property in St. James's.

There is always a sense of occasion about Joanna's work. She has a tremendous joie de vivre coupled with an effervescent personality to which people naturally gravitate. When she commissioned me to make furniture for the dining-room of a house in Hamilton Terrace, I remember her client had recently inherited some furs. 'Perfect!' Joanna said. 'Just what I need for the front hall!' She transformed the mink coats into fur stools. That sounds quite extraordinary, but it is a typical maverick turn.

Joanna is both very professional and great fun – a rare combination among designers – and notable for her use of craftsmen and furniture makers to achieve a bespoke interior for clients. As the following pages show, her priority is to create a place that is a home, not a show house. Mercurial in imagination, she not only knows the look and ambience she wants to achieve, but she also thinks through the practicalities of everyday life. I remember her interior designing the contents of a fridge on the final day of a project so that the owners could walk into their house and find everything as if it had always been there. She pays incredible attention to detail as well as beautifully made things.

As an interior designer she controls the overall vision of a project; from the very early days she showed me her vision of space, where the space shades of light go and how people live. I have learnt an incredible amount from her. She is very clear about what she wants, about budget and direction, which takes a lot of stress out of trying to achieve the best result for her client. It is always a great honour to see LINLEY work in her schemes.

The St James's project, which features in the last chapter of this book, is a summation of her talents. The undertaking involved both the restoration of a property – that is, an engineering exercise and a heritage exercise – as well as finding a simple common design language to make this vast space look and feel right. The result showcases Joanna's talents perfectly. It pleases the traditionalists while accommodating all the necessary accoutrements for modern life on an epic scale.

This wonderful book is an inspiration and delight that I feel appropriately illustrates the expertise and brilliance of one of our great British designers at the top of her game.

SUNNINGDALE

SUNNINGDALE

Houses designed in a particular era for an assumed lifestyle often retain an air of how they should be lived in, no matter how dilapidated they become or unsympathetically converted for modern use. This Victorian villa in Sunningdale, Berkshire, set in gloriously landscaped grounds overlooking the golf course, was built as a classic country home with a cricket-cum-polo pitch for an aristocrat who was attached to Queen Victoria's court at Windsor Castle and needed to live a mere carriage ride away.

Lord Westmoreland travelled extensively in Sri Lanka, Nepal and the Far East and became a fastidious collector of shrubs and plants on his odyssey. The house he commissioned has the long, low lines of a two-storey colonial bungalow – albeit on a grand scale – complete with white-columned entrance porch and verandah, pitched roofs and glorious shuttered windows overlooking a garden which begs to be strolled in or admired from a cushioned, wicker chair with a gin and tonic in hand. The very architectural bones of his lordship's 'cottage in the Queen's garden' call for happy family bustle, generous-spirited entertainment and the ultimate in domestic comfort.

My clients bought the property as a rundown retirement home. Ancient lino peeled from floors where once glorious rugs softened the wood underfoot; rows of institutional loos filled space once adorned by antique furniture; the grand, airy drawing room with its triple-faceted outlook onto the garden, had been divided into three poky rooms. The internal layout of the house was ruined although some decorative mouldings and certain architectural features had been retained. My brief was to return it to its original glory, unleash its joie de vivre and create a quintessential English country house that would have all the snug security of the ultimate, contemporary functioning family home.

The original architect was wonderfully generous with his windows. That was the thing that most struck me and the restoration architect, David Lloyd-Davis, on our initial site visit – light just pours in. One huge benefit about working on properties in the country is that there are no other buildings to block the sunlight. Here golden rays flood in at all angles, according to the time of day and the season. And of course, the windows afford many varied views out over the landscaped

Previous: *Bold drama comes from the rich, hand-painted aubergine stripes offset by the crisp white of the period mantelpiece, china and twinkling crystal.*
Far left: *The antique pulley chandelier illuminates only by candlelight. To add depth to the flickering light it radiates, we applied gloss varnish to the aubergine walls.*
Left: *With paintwork restored, my clients' childhood beds from the United States make a pretty guest bedroom pair.*

feature garden which we could see needed to be upgraded artfully for better year-round visual appeal. To celebrate this bountiful green setting, I was determined that an indoor/outdoor flow must be at the heart of the restoration dynamic. The garden must be the match of the house itself.

We worked on the sloping gardens with the distinguished landscape architect and designer Randle Siddeley. The aim was to showcase the beautiful avenue of rhododendrons at its centre and the shrubs that the original owner had brought back from his travels; we also wanted to create a balance between the house and its surroundings with new planting. The advantage of undertaking interior and exterior restoration in tandem is that planting can also be chosen to screen and diffuse any architectural disparities as well as to enhance the garden views. Here, a modern swimming pool wing had been built onto the main house without much care for architectural sympathy. Randle softened the harsh lines by planting a line of pleached lime trees and a low box hedge which beautifully break up the solid mass of brick and roof.

An indoor/outdoor scheme is all about vistas and blurring the interior/exterior divide so that outdoor spaces can double up as entertaining spaces when the weather allows. The grand terrace and the pool terrace provide ample room for outdoor dining, afternoon tea and summer cocktails. Gentle stone stairs lead down from the main colonnade onto the terrace, and more steps take you down again onto a path bordered by wisteria and hundreds of agapanthus mixed with lavender and spiked by cypress trees. Randle replaced the existing paving with creamier yellow York paving stones but reused the original stone to replace the perilously steep and unsightly steps that descended from the swimming pool terrace with an elegant fan of wide steps. These in turn lead to a flight of turf steps with stone treads to signify the transition from the formality of the terrace planting to the informality of this part of the garden.

I love floral fabrics when used in the right place. They can be a strong foil to a gorgeous exterior and a wonderful opportunity to release your inner romantic exuberance. If you had everything plain and neutral inside, the room would be very insipid. Here I used flower-patterned fabrics to mirror the stunning horticulture beyond the window panes; it was also historically in keeping. The phrase 'quintessential English country house' conjures up images of floral linens and chintzes. It epitomises the best of the formal but relaxed English Country House style, as it is difficult to make it look messy.

When you walk into the hall from the front door you can see all the way to the back of the house, to the French windows which open out onto one end of the verandah – from the minute you arrive your eye is drawn through to the garden. The hall still

Right: Quintessential English 'country house': the light, fresh colours in the drawing room are inspired by the Bennison printed floral linen on the sofas and echoed by the antique Aubusson rug.

Left: *An indoor/outdoor scheme is all about vistas and blurring the divide so that garden terrace spaces can double up as entertaining rooms when the weather allows.*

Above: *The walls are stippled in the palest lime green – a lovely neutral background for the antiques and vintage needlepoint we sourced to create a 'heritage' feel.*

had its original, wonderfully intricate Arts-and-Crafts-style mantelpiece: an eye-catching piece of inlaid woodwork with recessed frieze panels and carved relief details. I commissioned David Linley to make a complementary hall table, console and mirror to go en suite with this original fireplace and give unity to the space. The Arts and Crafts Movement was a clarion call for individual craftsmen to show off their skills, and the mix of woods – ebony, burr walnut, rosewood and satinwood – adds an elegant organic dimension to the hall.

I am a great believer in a hall having a flow and an aura in its own right. A strong design statement can add drama or set the tone of the house. I wanted to make this hall the warm, welcoming heart of the house. You approach the front door from under the portico and walk in under the lofty first-floor landing of the curving staircase, so you are immediately cocooned in your host's lair. Even the corkscrew spindles of the rich, pine staircase – which we discovered when we stripped away the institutional boxing – add a soft, embracing touch. The walls are papered in a muted pattern; deep-rose coloured upholstery projects hospitality and cheer in the seating arrangement in front of the fire. The hall can be used as a sitting room just as much as a thoroughfare. I imagine the Sunday papers laid out here, or guests having a drink before a winter lunch party, or random groups gathered as part of the in-and-out ebb and flow of a garden party on the veranda.

The large drawing room is to the right, off the hall. This room was possibly the most dramatic of 'before and after' scenarios, as we transformed what had been a mess of partitions, cramped meeting rooms and a cluster of loos back into a magnificently pretty room. With its wide bay window at the front, a pair of floor-to-ceiling French windows at the back and a further two windows on the long wall, it conjures up an air of grand yet relaxed colonial lifestyle. Light floods the space, cutting through at various angles throughout the day. The walls are pale green and the colour scheme is resolutely English floral abundance. On the twin sofas facing each other in front of the fireplace, I used a gorgeous Bennison pink and soft green lily print on ivory linen. Having selected the main pattern, I worked from that palette when adding another sofa and further chairs, cushions, throws and cool ivory lampshades edged with complementary petal pink, leaf green and neutral trimmings.

So many windows means plenty of curtains. The challenge was to allow the window frames to be gently draped with cool, quiet, elegant ivory silk and topped with gently swooping swags and pelmets in a weight that would suit the house, the architecture and the client without compromising the natural light in any way. To describe window dressing in fashion terminology, we were aiming for the equivalent of a floaty summer dress rather than a heavily-structured, rigid ballgown.

I have an armoury of tricks to help project an English country heirloom feel. I like to buy urns and antique vases to turn into lamps. Here, picking out the same garden colours, I also bought antique needlepoints and textiles to make cushions to scatter, adding texture and heritage. The needlepoint rug is

a calm, neutral background dotted with a large, gentle, floral garland pattern. The clients brought their own grand piano and I otherwise acquired antique furniture from dealers and salerooms; I also helped to put together a complementary collection of art. There is nothing reproduction under this roof.

The ambience of the drawing room is deeply soothing and comfortable. Every cushion is luxuriant feather and down; you sink into the sofa and chairs hoping not to have to hop out again very soon. I love the way the card table is always ready for a game of bridge or Scrabble. The clients have young children, entertain a lot and truly enjoy using their house. That family zeal for life permeates every inch of the property.

Dining rooms today are often multipurpose and clients opt for something fairly neutral to preserve the versatility. However, it is fun to be bold when you have the luxury of maintaining your dining room purely as a formal entertaining space. I love a dark dining room lit by candles for night-time entertaining – especially when you have a bright light kitchen for informal family eating. My client, who has a great sense of how to entertain with panache, was refreshingly daring about colour options. We came up with this drop-dead gorgeous, dark aubergine scheme. Purple is a complex colour with a range of associations, from regal to mystical, romantic to powerful, Gothic to fruits of the forest confection. I think the dept of colour here is pretty intrepid and the stripes add both formality and bravura. Hand painting stripes is a trick I often use because you can adjust the width of a stripe by just a few millimetres to ensure a symmetrical effect and to achieve the perfect pattern around a corner or window frame. Offset by the crisp white of the mantelpieces and the paintwork – and accessorised with white candles, flowers and china – the deep aubergine is dramatic, unusual and rather majestic. It makes for a bona fide special occasion room. The lovely antique crystal

Far left: An English country house demands a four-poster bed. Here, a number of dress elements combine to create a romantic, comfortable private sanctuary.
Top left: A cast-iron free-standing bath with Persian rug and French armchair combines functionality with luxurious comfort.
Bottom left: We restored two matching antique washstands with new marble. Mirrors sit slightly proud on the wall, concealing two medicine cupboards, to preserve the sense of space.

chandelier is on a pulley and illuminates only by candlelight. As a final flourish, we applied gloss varnish to the aubergine walls to bounce back the flickering light.

The kitchen is one area of the house we would transform to be very different from that of Lord Westmoreland's day. A Victorian house of this size would have had a separate kitchen, pantry, scullery, cellar and servants' rooms situated a corridor away from the reception rooms, with a retinue of servants to prepare and serve the food. Today cooking and catering is a social activity that requires an open-plan design. What family does not live in their kitchen? Modern life and informal entertaining is based around the kitchen, where family members and friends gravitate to read papers, scavenge for food, attempt homework or crosswords, prepare meals, write To Do lists and enjoy a cup of tea or glass of wine. You need space, and defined areas within that space, for food preparation and general loafing.

I took out three walls and brought back the space from smaller, non-original rooms to form a huge open-plan family room and kitchen. I left the central chimney breast so that you have a fireplace that opens both ways. It is an enormous but friendly space. When the fire is lit on a dark winter's day, it simultaneously livens up two living spaces. Any number of people can be engaged in separate activities, but within a universal buzz. The fairground horse on the kitchen side of the fire is a bit of fun, or, you might even say, an ironic comment on the merry-go-round of family life.

In contrast to the dining room, we installed a traditional working country kitchen with cream walls and units, wicker drawers and a lovely antique round table in Welsh oak with ladder-back chairs. We made two sets of slip cushion covers: deep rosy red to create warmth in the winter and lighter, half-pink, half-green checks for the summer months. The fabric for the blinds and curtains is a classic, bright Manuel Canovas floral print featuring blue china vases and fresh lemons – again to reach out and merge with the immediate garden area Randle had themed 'summery Mediterranean'. The blue vases in the fabric are echoed in the collection of blue teapots in the kitchen and in the blue glasses and vases on the other side of the chimney breast. Collections of teapots, china and earthenware jars with Winnie-the-Pooh honeypot glaze add a heritage, been-here-forever feel. I found a seventeenth-century Welsh oak dresser and chest to use in the sitting-room side of the room. A sturdy chest doubles up as an inexpensive coffee table and extra storage space for tablecloths, napkins and so on.

Nothing here is pretentious, just downright comfortable. For example, the centrepiece of 'his' library, in another room off the hall, is an old beaten-up chesterfield the client will never part with. A period library needs bones so we built in the English mahogany bookcases on either side of a polished French mantelpiece. We also installed library panelling, restored the cornices and skirting, and commissioned a desk from David Linley. The dark wood, rich colours and tartan chair and cushion covers evoke a masculine space for 'one man

Right: *A lovely, working country kitchen luxuriates in an organic feel with warm oak floors, cream walls and units, wicker drawers and antique Welsh oak table and ladder-back chairs.*
Far right: *The tiles above the Aga are hand-painted to echo the bright Manuel Canovas floral print which features blue china vases and fresh lemons.*

and his dog' – see the oil painting of a black hunting dog above fireplace! It is a room in which to put your feet up with the Financial Times and a glass of whisky – a true working/living space where the odd file or book out of place cannot ruin the integrity of the look.

Upstairs, the master bedroom is situated in a corner of the house and benefits from a double aspect over the garden. A traditional English country house demands a four-poster bed. Here we have created the ultimate vision of comfort, serenity and aesthetic appeal. Quite a number of dress elements – tenting, pelmets, bed skirts, canopy and trims – come together to create the elegant private enclosure about the four posts of beautifully turned mahogany, but again, it is both delicate in palette and weight to fit the light airy feel of the room.

We divided the next-door bedroom down the middle and produced 'his and hers' walk-in clothes closets with acres of space. With the bedroom in no danger of being buried under a clutter of clothes, it remains a sanctuary. I would love to hibernate here. Can you not imagine lying on a bank of pillows on the high bed and looking out to the treetops? Or taking comfort from a roaring fire in the fireplace off to the right? You can relax and put your feet up with a gripping book in the upholstered armchair in the corner, or sit and chat together in the romantic seating corner by the fire, under the gaze of Lady Hamilton, the mistress of Lord Nelson and muse of the artist George Romney.

The master bathroom conjures up comfort and functionality, but it is more of a room that happens to contain the wherewithal for bathing than one dominated by bathroom-ware. A cast-iron, free-standing bath is situated under the window. I painted the underside a lovely mid-blue and put an antique rug on the floor to go under the bath mat, creating a warmer, less functional feel. I found two matching antique washstands, restored them and redid the marble. We set the medicine cupboards into the wall behind the mirrors, so they sit only slightly proud on the wall and preserve the sense of space.

The guest bedroom is very pretty with a particularly harmonious colour scheme of aqua blue, green, grey and cream, led by the painted trim of the wooden beds. Like the treasured grand piano and chesterfield sofa downstairs, the pair of beds came over from the United States with the clients who have cherished them since childhood. That dynamic – of being inspired by the sense of 'life lived' both in the house itself and in items of the family's furniture – sums up our design ethos here.

Left: *The same design scheme extends to the other side of the double-sided fireplace in the open-plan kitchen, where the family sitting room is also furnished with an antique Welsh oak dresser, chest and table.*

Left: *A portrait of Picasso's studio hangs above the original intricate Arts and Crafts mantelpiece in the warm and welcoming hall.*
Above: *The fairground horse is a bit of fun or even an ironic comment on the merry-go-round of family life.*
Right: *The Linley console table and mirror commissioned to complement the Arts and Crafts mantelpiece. The mix of woods adds an elegant organic dimension to the hall.*

ASHBURTON HOUSE

A blank canvas is every designer's dream. Ashburton House, formerly a nineteenth-century stable and coach house, is now a seven-bedroom family house with a glamorous, contemporary interior. However, when I first saw the property it was a shell – a truly boring, low-ceilinged, dreary little house behind a wonderfully elegant, double-fronted facade. My aim was to conjure up an inside worthy of the magical outside.

The thrill for me was that the property required total transformation. When it was built in 1873 for Lady Ashburton, its four storeys were designed with input from her coachman. It was a house built for the comfort and convenience of horses, not humans. The ground floor comprised a coach house for several vehicles; a ramp led up to horse stalls on the first floor, above which was a balcony and a harness room. In 1910, it was converted into a garage and chauffeur's house; it underwent subsequent remodelling, but never with a family in mind.

I absolutely love space planning. A perfect Georgian mansion is easy but when space is tricky, it is much more inspiring. Once Ashburton House had been gutted, there were two important questions: Where should I put the staircase? (And what would it look like?) And how can I counter the problem of low ceilings and small windows? I would have to call upon my full armoury of light-reflecting and height-illusion tricks to make the eye work up and down.

With my team working alongside architects and contractors, we rebuilt the house, adding an extra floor at the top and extending down to create a basement level; we also installed a lift and staircase. My core principle is to get inside a client's head and instinctively work out how they live and how they aspire to live, and then endeavour to provide a home in which they are going to be happy. I reconsidered the layout of the house to incorporate the wish-list of air conditioning, a dining room, a drawing room, a media room to spend time with the kids, and seven bedrooms.

Some people can be extremely specific about details in their brief from the word go. For example, the female half of a couple might insist on having south-facing sunlight on her face when she sits at her dressing table in the morning, while her husband may want a drawer with a timed vibration device to activate the autowinds on his fabulous watch collection.

Previous: *A custom-made wave cabinet in exotic veneer houses a television and offers a fun counter focal point to the fireplace at the opposite end of the drawing room.*
Far left: *The arches are evocative of the building's origins as a coach house. We played on the symmetry with lanterns and trees to add to the grandeur.*
Left: *A patchwork hide rug creates an interesting motif on the floor and an unusual mirror provides 'eye candy'.*

They may have strong views on colour – confessing to an abhorrence of hot colours in favour of a neutral palette – or harbouring an antipathy to a certain kind of flooring. However, there were no such particular requests at Ashburton House. I was simply allowed to get on with it, from broadbrush strokes down to final details.

Deciding where in a house to position a staircase (and also, in this case, a parallel lift) is one of the most difficult things to do when space planning from scratch. Luckily the position of the lift was a given because of architectural constraints, so for a visual starting point I had a grand staircase and a lift together in the right rear corner of the property, with glorious light thrown down from a skylight above.

The next decision to make was where to put the dining room. I fixed on the space on the front left of the property, opening off the hall – a room which receives light from both sides and has an outlook onto a pretty courtyard. In the city, you are always hunting for light for the formal living rooms. When allocating space, you are working within planned parameters, arranging your jigsaw pieces. With the dining room position fundamental, the kitchen would be located at the back of the house.

I love a dark, moody hall opening out into a lighter staircase – it creates a sense of drama when visitors arrive. If the colour tone is all the same, the effect is one-dimensional and it does not embrace you. I am always looking to create space in a hall, as the area inside the front door can fill up quickly, whether it is with schoolbags or Prada bags. If the area is well designed, it becomes great circulation space. I always like a mirror too, because an entrance hall is often a dark or tight space. A mirror, such as the pretty leaf-filigree circular frame here, attracts light and provides 'eye candy'. I aim for every room to have something gorgeous or flamboyant for the eye to feast on. Quite often it can be a single piece of art or sculpture, or a vignette; it could be a magnificent functional item such as a circular bath, a bold mixture of colours or a combination of these things.

So the layout was sorted out to make the space work best for the family: informal rooms in the basement (media room, gym, utility room and maid's bedsit), kitchen and dining room on the ground floor, and the formal drawing room and library on the first floor. The rest of the house would consist of the bedrooms, bathrooms and dressing rooms.

Right: *A gilded coffer with LED lights around the perimeter creates an impression of ceiling height. The mirrored wall adds depth. I like to bevel the edges of the glass panels for added interest.*

Left: *Note the oval motif, replicated in ceiling, table shape and rug. We created drama by upholstering a bold pattern on the back of the dining chairs.*

Low ceilings posed the main challenge in the formal rooms. In the hall, I countered this with a subtle sunken panel or 'coffer' within the neutral painted ceiling – this is very effective in lifting space. A dining room is unique because the focal point is always the middle of the room and that focus gave me the opportunity to create a strong harmonious central line which detracts from the low ceiling height. We applied a wonderful gold leaf paper in the oval coffered ceiling, illuminated by a tiny firmament of surround lights. This raises the space above the oval custom-made walnut table, which stands on an oval rug; the coloured centre section of the rug exactly mirrors the size of the coffered oval of the ceiling. From rug to table to ceiling, the eye is drawn upwards along the lines created by three repetitions of an oval within a square. Another trick here was to cut back the cornice above the windows so that the curtains go all the way from ceiling to floor, thereby lengthening the line.

It is vital in each room to think about when and how it is going to be used. A dining room is used more often at night, so I like to decorate to an appropriate night lighting level. We put in an entire wall of antiqued mirror, which beautifully reflects light bouncing off the lovely oval chandelier. I am keen on custom designing items because it gives individuality for the clients and I commissioned this chandelier to be delicate, fresh, light crystal, so it does not obstruct vision. The gold leaf paper on the ceiling is wonderfully reflective of crystal and candlelight. It is all about optical illusions.

Mindful of the budget, we put bold and expensive fabric on the back of the chairs but plain fabric on the front. We also had the rug made up with plain Wilton carpets, put together by our carpet makers, which is significantly cheaper than ordering a handmade rug.

The kitchen, with its bamboo cabinets, offers an eco-friendly, durable and easy-to-clean practicality. Starting with a light floor to create a sense of spaciousness, we mixed bamboo with a pale medium created by white lacquer panels, a white glass splashback and white Corian worktops. The glory of a glass splashback is that it is one piece, so it has no cracks to collect gunk and it picks up the light very well. Bamboo has created a bit of a 'green' frisson in interior design, as it is fast growing, rapidly renewable and surprisingly tougher than most hard woods. I love the idea of using a sustainable source.

Left: *To use space efficiently in the office I designed a built-in desk as part of the fitted furniture. Comfortable seating provides the setting for informal meetings. Note the contemporary take on a wing chair for a maverick touch.*

Left: *Sleek simplicity: the handle-less kitchen doors by Kitchenhaus have veneers of sustainable caramel bamboo. The 'legless' Corian table is supported on a hidden bracket to give the impression it is floating with no apparent support.*

Staircases can convey both drama and elegance. The staircase here holds a lot of appeal. The continuous curve is beautiful on the eye and cleverly worked with the service pipes boxed neatly and invisibly into the apex of the walls. Running up six storeys from the basement to the roof under natural light, it creates a tremendous feeling of space and airiness.

Sometimes it is effective to standardise materials all the way through a property. For example, the wood used in the staircase is walnut. You see it throughout Ashburton House in the floors, panelling, inlays, doors and cabinets – and in the relatively simple walnut panel and mirror interior of the lift. Coherence of design and a natural fluidity is important to me. I am not an advocate of the bitty, paintbox approach to rooms. I could see the potential for a fluid first-floor arrangement of drawing room, library/study and bar and that has worked extremely well. I like opening spaces one into the next – a space within a space. The two rooms can work together or separately. The space would be less functional if it was one small room leading off a slightly bigger one with an awkward corner. To maximise space we again opted for coffered recessing, with moulding and lines of lights around the coffers. Walnut features in the joinery and in the floors to maintain a coherent feel – I prefer floors and rugs to fitted carpets because it creates an illusion of space. We designed a coffee table in glass and nickel, adding more reflection and light to further open out the room.

Right: *The bones of the scheme in this pretty and feminine girl's room work so that the client can easily update with accessories as the child grows older and goes through different phases.*

The fireplace is the focal point of the drawing room. Opposite, I have balanced it with more eye candy - a stunning, custom-made wave cabinet in an exotic veneer, which houses a television. It is a fun, dramatic, counter-focal point. I like going for a colour scheme that provides quiet background. Here we chose a buttermilk cream for the walls and curtains – not too claustrophobic – and created interest with blocks of colour, cutting the neutral backdrop with a warm, contrasting palette of dusky grey and violet through to dark burgundy, worked through in the lampshades, lamp bases, veneers, cushions and roll-up faux crocodile leather stool.

When decorating with a simple colour palette, texture is incredibly important. Here, cushions covered in sumptuous velvet, smooth eelskin and shimmering silk serve as contrast to the sofas, which are upholstered in a plain woven fabric. By offsetting texture against texture, you highlight the appealing characteristics of different materials. That is why trims are so important: because of the counterpoint.

Further harmony is attained from the mellow colours in the embroidered textile on the chairs and in the beautifully faded antique Persian rug. On the walls we hung two wonderful photographs of opera house interiors by Candida Höfer, who is famed for capturing the essence or soul of national institutions; they are terribly decorative, but also convey an extraordinary sense of perspective.

Right: *Wall brackets set on to the mirror maximise light. I like china bathroom fittings in any colour - as long as it's white.*
Below: *Polished plaster: the guest bathroom owes its lustrous sheen to a 16th-century Italian technique, stucco Veneziano.*

To make fun use of otherwise dead space, we filled an awkward corner with a funky curved bar, adorned in pearlised purple vinyl. With its art deco ocean liner associations, the bar creates visual interest as well as an extra seating spot; it also provides a practical area for glasses and coffee pots within an entertaining space.

The study adjoining the drawing room is a functioning workspace that doubles as a sitting room. Again, it is an L-shape, so we used the smaller tangent for built-in joinery and the desk, specifically to set it apart from the seating area. The modern world increasingly works from home. That is particularly the case with foreigners who have business interests in London, and an important element in an office now is to incorporate a sitting area. In some cultures, sitting on either side of a desk suggests a hierarchy. The younger generation prefers not to conduct business from behind piles of papers but more face-to-face. Most people like to sit on the same side of a table, perhaps to look at a screen together, so I am careful to incorporate the new nuances of evolving work manners into room design.

We have picked up the same colour palette against the walnut, accentuating the deeper claret tones in the rug and high-backed armchair for a more masculine flavour. The overall effect of the room is that it feels intimate at night, but not too dark during the day. It is functional but aesthetically pleasing, with all unsightly computer and technology clobber hidden away. I am always working hard to make wires disappear.

The second floor is comprised of three guest bedrooms and their en-suite bathrooms. Again, low ceilings and the need for air conditioning presented major challenges, but I think cocooned spaces make cosy bedrooms. My mission with guest bedrooms is to make them as comfortable as possible, with great bathrooms. You want guests to enjoy their room and feel able to sit, nest, rest, bathe and spread their stuff around. The three rooms are different in personality – a girl's bedroom, a green and grey toned room and a slightly more masculine scheme in camel and blue – but all are decorated over a quiet, calm, standardised neutral background. In the little girl's room I designed a sweet but sophisticated pink and green scheme so that the room can grow and evolve with the child with no need to redecorate through every age phase.

Left: *A serpentine-fronted chest of drawers maximises storage while creating the illusion of space and fluid flow around a small room. A comfortable chair without arms is another de-cluttering trick.*

Left: *The drawing room required all the tricks to counter a low ceiling. I used low-backed sofas with button detail to focus attention and we cut back cornices to extract every last centimetre of height for the pelmet and curtains.*

The big guest bathroom owes its glow to a polished plaster effect I love to use: stucco Veneziano (Venetian plaster), which has a lovely sheen and is thoroughly waterproof. It is a sixteenth-century Italian technique in which a pre-tinted plaster is applied in thin layers and trowelled to a highly-polished, cold, marble-like lustre. The underfloor heating goes on like an electric blanket. I am a great believer in being warm and snug in a bathroom.

Another light-reflecting effect I like in a bathroom is used in the mother-of-pearl tiled panel in the guest shower room. It looks very attractive with the lights. I also had a custom-made square shower tray cut in honed marble – much nicer than a ready-made standard ceramic tray – and saved costs by mixing the real McCoy, the Thassos marble, with cheaper Denver White. The combination not only reduces costs but lifts the look into something more special.

The airy ceiling height on the top floor is much more generous for the master bedroom. An ivory colour scheme, absolutely neutral, immediately gives a contemporary feel. They say the best way to teach an artist is to paint in monochrome, because you have to get the details right to make it work. When everything is cream, white, beige or ivory, the texture, trims and decorative details become ultra-important as a way of creating interest away from colour. Despite my own natural inclination towards colour, I find this an immensely peaceful room.

I like putting texture on walls. Here I have applied a paper-backed, linen-silk mixture to give a neutral but opulent feel. The ivory carpet with integral diamond pattern gives warmth and luxury. The oversized padded headboard in cream suede (which had to be made in pieces to get it into the room) adds a further indulgent dimension above the large, two meter square, commodious bed. In the bedding and cushions, there are lots of different textures and trimmings within the ivory palette to create a warm and soft ambience. This is offset by the hard lines of the chimney breast, mantel and mirror. I am a huge admirer of Sir John Soane and we have used a lovely Soane-style mantelpiece with an oversized mirror embraced by a pair of witty, elongated, dramatic lights to accentuate the calming height of the room. We had fun playing with the up-and downsizing contrasts in this room.

My mantra is to think about the use of the room: a dressing table for make-up or writing, a comfy seating area to sit in front of the fire, a bed with a bank of pillows on which to relax and watch television, capacious storage space, and plenty of eye candy on the walls in the form of arty photographs. It is the ultimate comfort, I think, to have a fire in the bedroom. It creates a homely perspective and makes the room an alluring, personal retreat.

Walnut recurs in the furniture to continue the unifying theme so the eye is not exhausted by lots of different woods. We have used walnut in a variety of ways, including the chests, which are custom-made in burr walnut. The curve of the bow-fronted furniture is a softening touch with feminine appeal; we have also conjured up cream lacquer bedside cabinets in fun, feminine shapes. I do not like to waste any space; I like bedside tables to have shelves, drawers – functionality. We also had a piece of furniture constructed to take a flat-screen television at the end of the bed.

We put the dressing room into the dormer space – potentially a tricky space to work, but the variety of options for storage shelves and drawers helps to cope with the slant and make each inch work as useful space. In a townhouse, space is at a premium. When just one square foot in Knightsbridge costs £3,000, every inch has to work. By maximising space within the slant and installing adjustable shelves in cupboards and wardrobes, you can create a pretty and useful arrangement of storage space. I used the area under the dormer window for a dressing table, not just for the light, but to make practical use of dead space. Pretty maple veneer is used inset in the drawer fronts, with fun knobs to upgrade the overall feel of luxury.

My mission is to make people feel comfortable and pampered. It is critical to have sockets for the hairdryer or straighteners. I might incorporate a suede-lined drawer for jewellery and cufflinks. I try to second-guess everything, creating interesting and surprising features, which even my clients had not thought they would need.

Bathrooms should be somewhere you relax. I adore louvre shutters, as opposed to blinds or curtains, as they let in light but maintain privacy. I also like cupboards, so that everything can be put away. I hate there not being enough storage – why not use every inch of space? Above the loo, for example, I have adorned the wall with a glass shelved display cabinet.

The basement features a media room for the family, with a sprung wooden floor so that you can roll back the rug and set

JOANNA WOOD

out yoga mats, or, in another phase of life, install a home gym. The sprung floor gives versatility, but with hard flooring you have to be mindful of acoustics. A rug with a good underlay, combined with fabric-covered walls, is a good softening device. In a television room I am a great believer in putting in lovely, squashy, L-shaped seating. If there are two of you, you can lie out; if there are eight or ten of you, you can still sit comfortably. Daylight is not an issue in an entertainment room. A dark and dreary space becomes an amusement zone. I sometimes do dark colours for a cinema-like atmosphere, but since this room doubles as a gym, I have continued with the neutral background with splashes of strong, uplifting colour. Fun continues with the yin and yang run-up stools on coasters, which are ideal to pull up for a big game of Monopoly or for simply putting your feet up.

The rest of the lower floor comprises a utility room, a cellar, the engine rooms, the maid's bedsit, and a corner for the ironing board. I am always thrilled when I find a place for the ironing board!

TIPS

- Stucco Veneziano, a technique of applying polished plaster, first used in the sixteenth century, creates a surprisingly affordable and practical luxurious sheen on bathroom walls. Plenty of plaster specialists carry out this type of finish for projects small or large.
- A mixture of bona fide marble with affordable marble can reduce costs and lift the look of a bathroom.
- Add Swarovski crystal doorknobs to raise an ordinary cupboard or chest of drawers into something extraordinary with an element of sparkle and grandeur.
- A great trick to disguise low ceilings is to cut back the cornice above windows and run curtains from the ceiling to the floor.

Left: *A resolutely neutral, ivory colour scheme gives a contemporary feel to the master bedroom. Without colour to play with, the texture, trims and decorative details create the interest. An oversized padded headboard in cream suede (which had to be made in pieces to get it into the room) adds a further indulgent dimension.*

Left: *I designed the basement media room with a neutral background and a sprung wooden floor so that the space can double up as a gym - roll back the rug and you can set out yoga mats and fitness equipment. I am a great believer in lovely, squashy, L-shaped seating in an entertainment room and the yin and yang run-up stools on coasters are ideal to pull up for a big game of Monopoly.*

KENSINGTON TOWN HOUSE

Restoration often goes hand in hand with pushing the boundaries in interior design. Behind an icing-sugar white, stucco Victorian facade, this Kensington townhouse is now the quintessential mix of classic and contemporary. Originally built between 1855 and 1870 as a smart family home run on an 'Upstairs, Downstairs' dynamic, that is, with the servants living downstairs and the family upstairs, before it fell into reduced circumstances between the wars and was converted into flats. My brief was to remodel it as a glamorous family house with all the twenty-first-century domestic toys: gym, pool, home spa, cinema and so on, incorporating the latest audiovisual technology and mechanics.

In order to achieve that I first had to 'clean up', rediscovering the property's classic outlines and reinstating the correct architectural detailing. This meant researching and sourcing everything from antique mantelpieces and period cornices to columns and marble floors, so that the bones of the house were sympathetic to the original idiom. Only then could I set about adjusting it for contemporary living. We reinstated a sweeping staircase and dug down to excavate a double basement.

As well as the big-picture remodelling, it was important to work on the structural trimmings. Early on I needed to establish the hierarchy of proportion between cornice, skirting, architraves and door dimensions so that we could confirm a design discipline that would run throughout the house. For example, we built in broad skirting in the hall but reduced the skirting height on the top bedroom floor by half. We had to ensure the proportions of the associated details remained the same when the sizes were scaled down as you went up the floors and the ceiling heights gradually lowered.

The entrance hall of a property on this scale demands an air of grandeur, especially when it is home to a family for whom lavish entertaining is important. When a visitor arrives at a house set back from the road behind smart iron railings and a landscaped front garden, and climbs up to its imposing front door via an impressive flight of steps, they have to step into a hall that lives up to the approach. I put in pairs of classical columns to dramatise the space leading into the hall from the vestibule, and we laid a stunning limestone floor with black marble keystones. The black marble was copied into the columns using a technique called scagliola, where ground marble is applied and highly polished. It came into fashion in seventeenth century Tuscany as a substitute for expensive

Previous: *The entrance hall makes a grand statement about perspective, courtesy of the photograph and palette. A gorgeously wacky chandelier of glass baubles hangs like a luxuriant bunch of berries above a circular table in a variety of hues that feature throughout the ground floor.*
Far left: *Dramatic intent: we installed wonderful black scagliola columns on marble plinths to separate the lobby from the hall.*
Left: *A property on this scale demands an entrance of grandeur.*

marble inlays but it is a rarefied practice today – only three craftsmen in Europe are skilled in this particular technique. The result is gleaming stone that bounces light around so you are immediately struck by a sense of elegant spaciousness.

I like an entrance hall to make an immediate design statement. Once the classic lines were reinstated, I introduced our striking, contemporary focal points: a pair of black lamps on a modern console inside the vestibule, and more theatrically in the hall, a gorgeously wacky chandelier of glass baubles which hangs like a luxuriant bunch of grapes above a circular table. The glass was especially blown in a variety of berry colours – raspberry through to blueberry, via prune, pink, claret and red – which is the palette that features throughout the ground floor. Visually, the chandelier works like an overture that precedes an opera. Your brain subconsciously registers a decorative theme that will be played out on a more extensive and dramatic scale as you move through the rooms.

The kitchen and breakfast room is on the left of the hall, in the space that would traditionally have been a library or morning room. It was bold to turn the main front room into a 'working' room, e.g. the kitchen, which would traditionally have been hidden downstairs or at the back of a grand house; however, playing with the layout was part of the contemporariness here. In many ways, kitchens have not changed in well over a hundred years. Our minds are hidebound by the cupboard module – we have been brainwashed into accepting the line of units as the standard look for a kitchen. What I like to do is innovate, to think how people live and to reflect that in my designs. A kitchen is now more of a living space than a working space. Cooking has become part of our social life. Who does

not live and entertain in their kitchen nowadays? Even rich, young people like to be informal (and in a house of this scale, there may well be a catering kitchen downstairs for serious food production).

In this classic, architecturally formal space – a main reception in a period house – we 'floated' a cool kitchen in a white Corian frame so that it retained its own identity and functionality, without interfering with the architectural lines. Glamour is inherent in the sleekness of the beautiful rosewood units, which are in high gloss with white Corian countertops, glass splashbacks and counter front panels. The sofa-style banquette in the bay window is upholstered in tactile raspberry suede; it makes a chic but comfortable sitting area, perfect for hosting friends for coffee or a light lunch, for providing children with a grazing-cum-homework area or for casual kitchen suppers. A two-level counter means that unless you are on the business side of the work surface, you never see the mess.

Flexibility is the key in designing contemporary living space. I am a big advocate of installing different lighting options to change the mood and usage of a room. Here we installed LEDs to project funky pink and moody blue neon lighting from behind the glass splashbacks, glass counter front panels and wall shelving. When lit up in this very sophisticated way, the room can be closed down as a kitchen and opened up as an international bar-cum-nightclub! It is a canny way to create extra entertaining space. We put bar seats around two sides of the counter, on the corner next to the cocktail cabinet; that way, guests can pick up their Martini cocktail and float through into the drawing room.

Flow is key in a multi-functional entertaining space. At 750 square feet (70 square metres), the adjacent grand, formal drawing room is very large and stretches back to a stunning, rounded bay window. French windows open out directly onto the garden and double sliding doors lead to the dining room. It is a huge space and instinctively I wanted to create three cosy seating groups that could work together or separately. Two of the seating areas are on opposite sides of the rooms, but not symmetrically facing. To create warmth and intrigue in the layout, the left-hand side of the room works horizontally along the wall, based around a long, capacious sofa and attendant armchairs, a low glass table and upholstered stools. A triptych of photographs of ornate cavernous opera house interiors by my favourite artist, Candida Höfer, conveys depth on this long, flat wall. Facing this arrangement but slightly offset, is another seating area in a more formal setting: two chaises longues sandwiching a coffee table, perpendicular to the fireplace.

When you walk into the room, however, your attention is drawn to the amazing bay window at the end which gives a panoramic outlook over the lovely garden. Led by the roundness of the window, I positioned an old-fashioned conversation chair in the centre of the space in front of it (a multi-backed, round upholstered stool on which historically groups of women sit and gossip). I completed the sense of an open, circular 'room within a room' with the position of two chic armchairs. The mood is light and airy with a natural feel. In this space I have used less colour and pattern as it was important not to intrude upon the glorious view through to the garden. The chairs have low arms, curved like a scimitar; the curtains are neutral and hang straight in regular, column-shaped gatherings and overhead light shines from a delicate, tapered chandelier above the conversation chair. The attractions here are the windows and the view they afford.

Left: *To create warmth and intrigue in the vast drawing room that stretches back to a rounded bay window, I designed three cosy seating groups that could work together or separately.*

This drawing room is a good example of living at a level of contemporary luxury in a period framework. On top of neutral walls and cream rugs on parquet floors, the overall decorative feel is a medley of harmoniousness. Layering on top of a neutral background is my trademark; I love the process of creating interest and a warm, enveloping elegance by playing on a chosen colour palette in textiles, cushions, table lamps and furnishings.

The same neutral scheme extends through to the dining room, which is dominated by a rectangular table that seats fourteen but can stretch to twenty. This room is super symmetrical: the mantelpiece, chandelier and table are positioned precisely to parallel the wall configuration of twin console tables topped with identical round mirrors on either side of the fireplace. Most rooms are better with a form of symmetry somewhere. I always start with symmetry and break out; that philosophy is a good basis for planning. However, be aware that perfect symmetry can be quite clinical and cold. Here I added red-hot flowers and colourful china to augment the warm tones of the chairs and create some 'heat'. The rectangular chandelier was commissioned to fill the space above the rectangular table and also to provide a centre light. Rooms used exclusively for formal dining call for a central focus.

Reinstating a handsome staircase was a particularly gratifying element of this project. Who knows, we could have inherited a chunky flight of stairs that turned a rigid ninety degrees at a time but instead, we had the opportunity to install a sweeping stone staircase that is graceful in its gentle escalation. Each floor has a spacious landing which benefits from light coming from the sky above and from lateral sunlight shining through stepped pairs of windows. Staircase interiors in London rarely have windows, but here was an opportunity to add prettiness with a series of blinds whilst filtering the outlook to the next-door neighbours' brick wall. Landings on this scale are a luxury but spaces that are not used are just as important as ones that are. If I had to pick a cameo of my trademark style, this first-floor landing would be it. I absolutely love the combination of the gilt and marble Louis XVI console and the zingy, green and white Caio Fonseca painting.

Left: *A four-seater sofa, attendant armchairs and upholstered stools are arranged around a low coffee table to form one seating group.*
Above: *Room within a room: a traditional conversation chair and custom-made chandelier marks the centre of the circular space led by the rounded bay window.*
Right: *A perfect cameo of contemporary meets classic: two chaise longues sandwich a coffee table in a formal fire-side setting.*
Overleaf: *Super-symmetry: red-hot flowers and colourful china by William Yeoward create 'heat' amid the precise positioning of mantelpiece, chandelier and table to parallel the wall configuration of twin console tables and mirrors.*

The air of sumptuous serenity in the master bedroom comes from a combination of elements: the layered soft furnishings; the colour palette of dusky pink, rose and violet; the pretty dressing table; and an intimate seating arrangement around the fireplace. There is no danger of clutter ruining the orderly aura as the vast floor space allows for adjacent his-and-hers bathrooms, dressing rooms, and even a study for the master of the household. Increasingly I am asked by international clients with several homes to replicate their main personal study, right down to layout, furniture, computer and pen pots; this is so they can stealthily nip out of bed to deal on the markets in the small hours with minimum disturbance and operate on autopilot.

Left: *Layered soft furnishing in a dusky pink and violet palette create an air of sumptuous serenity.*
Below: *The pretty custom-made dressing table adds to the orderly aura.*

The highlight of this floor is the master bathroom. You walk through the main dressing room – where lines formed by shelves behind thick, glass panels and a series of mirrors combine to create an ultra-glamorous, infinity effect – into a spectacular, octagonal bathroom. The design was inspired by the construct of the bay window. The window gave us three sides of an octagon, so we were led by the architectural lines and completed the shape, echoing it into a coffered ceiling and keeping the shower, loo and cupboards behind the octagonal sides. The large white bath sits invitingly as the focal point of a room trimmed with subtle bespoke finishes, including details such as mother-of-pearl drawer handles.

The second and third floors comprise seven more bedrooms, each with their own bathrooms; the house is truly ambassadorial in scale. I particularly like the pastel-toned guest suite which is gently pretty and universally appealing. It feels like a welcoming nest despite its clean, grand proportions; the soft, light monochrome patterned wallpaper depicts a feathery backdrop and the mirrored furniture radiates light softened by the gauzy window dressing. In the bathroom we have picked out the eau de Nil of the bed headboard and dressing table chair in striking stripes. Stripes also feature in the other two bedrooms on the second floor: on the sofa in the girl's

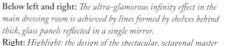

Below left and right: The ultra-glamorous infinity effect in the main dressing room is achieved by lines formed by shelves behind thick, glass panels reflected in a single mirror.
Right: *Highlight: the design of the spectacular, octagonal master bathroom was inspired by the architectural lines of the bay window.*

Far left: *The study was designed to replicate the layout of the main study in my client's other homes – right down to identical furniture, computer and pen pot.*
Left: *The alcove under a window was utilised to provide additional space in a gentleman's dressing room.*
Below: *Supremely stylish yet practical, David Linley Garrick desk accessories in walnut with sycamore marquetry include a flat blotter, square pencil pots, noteholder and letter rack and provide the final decorative flourish in the study.*

bedroom, in the form of eye-catching orange and powder pink upholstery, and in the blue and white nautical stripes of the boy's bathroom. Here I have employed one of my favourite tricks by painting broad stripes to set them out from the corner.

The playground zones – which elevate this property to the 'home with everything' – begin on the lower ground floor. Under its double-height ceiling, it comprises an extensive swimming pool with sauna and steam room, a jacuzzi, a massage area, showers and a changing area, as well as a gym and an informal sitting room with the mother of all televisions. The concept of a home spa, with all the pampering toys, has evolved in its look and facilities and in its potential as living space. I like to design spa areas as entertaining rooms, with strategically subtle lighting-as-art effects, rather than as private

utilities. I imagine convivial, poolside Sunday brunches or a gathering of teenagers lolling on the cushioned, rattan seats or perhaps a Gatsby-esque summer cocktail party in full swing.

A spa complex is made up of lots of little rooms adjoining the main pool area, so it is incredibly important to consider circulation. Part of the rest-and-relaxation vibe comes from the feeling that you can waft through to the garden or into the family room or back upstairs. The swimming pool has double doors leading into both the family room and the garden terrace. We chose Scandinavian pine to create a natural feel, mindful of the fact that – weather permitting – the family will want to extend out on to the gorgeous terrace. As an indoor pool can easily induce claustrophobia, I strive to create an illusion of brightness and freshness. The walls and floor are a warm neutral and we installed big, glass ceilings as skylights so that the pool feels as under the open sky as possible. Japanese-inspired, semi-opaque glass screens divide the pool from the

gym and from the family room; understated and chic, they also help to get light in every which way.

When it comes to standards, I always want a spa to be as clean as a hospital and as comfortable as the most luxurious resort. I expect fluffy towels, warm heating and chilled champagne. The pool is lined with cream which gives it a lovely, soft, aqua-green colour instead of that harsh, rather dated, bright turquoise. Horizontal lines in different media and different shades within the decoration scheme all match up throughout the spa area, so it is unifying and harmonious to the eye. We kept going with this design statement to pull together the variety of spaces in the layout; we called upon bright blue, aqua and navy where we needed injections of colour, such as in the changing room, the snazzy loo, and on cushions.

From this floor, you go truly, madly, deeply underground to the sub-basement. It is too far underground for formal living space but perfect for those all-important lifestyle rooms

Left and right: *An Indoor/Outdoor dynamic is critical to my interiors. The task of creating 'rooms' outside is particularly important in a city. Here, the rectangular form of the skylights, which illuminate the swimming pool in the spa below, provide rug-shaped spaces around which we placed outdoor seating.*

that do not require daylight. The feature room on this level is a spectacular home cinema which comfortably seats twelve in tiered seating covered in squidgy, Missoni-esque fabric cushioning. Strategically placed, square stools await wine buckets and popcorn. Next to the cinema is a temperature-controlled, glass-encased wine vault which stores more than a thousand bottles. It is not just state-of-the-art in terms of technology, it is also a thing of beauty in the way it displays the collection of bottles. Better still, it is ideally situated for opening a bottle of chilled Chablis before taking your seat for the matinée.

The rest of the floor houses the nuts and bolts of life: utility room, catering kitchen and plant machinery for the pool and sauna complex. But the fun does not end inside the house

Left: *A stunning home cinema, the feature room in the sub-basement level, comfortably seats twelve in tiered seating covered in Missoni-esque fabric which is warm in texture and tone. Note the square stools strategically placed for wine buckets and popcorn.*
Below: *Next to the cinema is a state-of-the-art, temperature-controlled, glass-encased wine vault which stores more than a thousand bottles. Conveniently situated for opening a chilled Chablis before a screening, it is also a thing of beauty in the way its geometrically designed joinery displays the collection.*

– the imaginative use of the garden as a set of outdoor rooms also distinguishes this property. The front and rear gardens are designed by Stephen Woodhams, who has pioneered the 'inside/outside' concept since 1995. We worked together to create a series of relaxing outdoor spaces to link with the interior.

If you flew over the rear garden you would see it is arranged as if it were two rooms. The rectangular form of the skylights, that illuminate the swimming pool on the level below, resembles the shape of the soft, aqua-green rugs, around which we placed the seating arrangement. Timber decking is underfoot, while muted blues and lavender greys bring the ground floor colour palette out into the 'great outdoors'. This garden area opens out directly from the formal drawing and dining rooms. We placed a dining table and chairs on tiles to create the outdoor al fresco entertaining space.

To mirror the reinstated architectural lines inside the house, Stephen created walls and structure in the garden rooms too. Timber screens work as 'room' dividers, but also ingeniously cover all the extraction and filter systems for the basement swimming pool and air-conditioning units. Pleached hornbeam trees create a screen effect at the front of the house while, at the rear, four mulberry trees sit squarely in huge pots to add horticultural columns of linear height. A further sense of proportion emanates from the use of oversized, cream clay pots, planted with boxwood spheres, repeated in rows of three or five. Again, clever lighting-as-art effects act as mood changers between day and night.

Left and below: *Contributing to the horticultural architecture, Mulberry trees sit squarely in huge pots to add linear height and rows of boxwood spheres in oversized pots add a further sense of proportion.*

Above and right: *Working with garden designer Stephen Woodhams we created walls and structure with pleached hornbeam trees and timber screens to mirror the lines inside the house.*

TIPS

- Consider the impact of an entrance hall. I recommend dramatic decorations – a stunning chandelier, mirror or colour scheme – to make something special of a utilitarian space and set the scene for a decorative theme throughout the house.
- Establish a hierarchy of proportion between the structural trimmings by ensuring the proportions of cornice, skirting, architraves and door dimensions remain the same on each floor; you may need to adjust the dimensions as you go upstairs and ceiling heights typically lower.
- Think about how you can use space to encourage 'flow' from one room to another. For example, make a feature of a drinks cabinet in the kitchen next to the double doors that take you through to the drawing room.
- To unify and harmonise a space with lots of small open rooms, decorate with horizontal lines in different media and different shades of a colour so the eye is tricked into matching everything up.

JOANNA'S
BARN

An ancient cow barn is my family's country bolt-hole. Constructed from a mix of flint and brick, it was once part of a home farm to an Elizabethan estate and it is said that a barn has stood here since medieval times as part of a lively, agricultural homestead. The building has metamorphosed over the years into the five-bedroom haven to which we retreat for weekend and holiday relaxation. I love the fact that the site has been used by people for centuries. I sometimes sit in front of a huge, crackling fire and wonder what beam was added when.

It is always rewarding to work with the history of a period building to retain its character. We have seen old photographs that show a row of cows munching from the byre in the part of the barn that is now, quite aptly, our dining room. The barn would have started with a beaten earth floor and much later been laid with brick. In the immediate years before we moved in, the building had been spruced up considerably in order to be used as a location for shooting parties' lunches, so although it needed some structural work, we did not need to gut it. In a property with abundant natural features – such as the original flint and brick walls, beams and galleried upper level here – the aim is to be restrained in decorative style in order to highlight the inherent architectural interest.

Essentially, my task was a comprehensive redecoration. I wanted to keep the look simple and practical. For us, a family getaway means dogs, children, horses and the often muddy aftermath of long walks and rides across country. The house represents a change of tempo; a peaceful haven where we come to recover from our busy working week and restore ourselves for the next one, often in the company of friends. I certainly did not want anything too ornate; I wanted to make it feel like you can put your feet up on anything or even walk around in your wellingtons. Some people might put a few logs in a pretty wicker basket next to the fire and keep the bulk supply in an outhouse, but I think logs stacked up in an alcove alongside the fireplace look great aesthetically and also send out a welcoming come-hibernate-here signal. I am a great believer in the beauty of functionality. I may have cream slip covers for the dining chairs but they go straight into the washing machine, no problem.

In sympathy with the existing architecture, I had some of the woodwork restored and I replaced all the doors. Downstairs we laid a combination of wooden flooring in the kitchen and dining area, and practical sisal carpet over the rough stone floors throughout the rest of the ground floor (not

Previous and far left: *The beautiful replication of Jacobean embroidery in the fabric used to upholster this small prayer chair holds together the rich tones of the decorative scheme in the galleried drawing-room.*
Left: *I designed the interior to highlight the inherent architectural features of our ancient flint and brick cow barn.*

over beautiful farmhouse stone tiles, I hasten to add – this was more like agricultural concrete). I like hard floors. They are in every way the base layer of all my design schemes and in a large room, such as the galleried drawing room here, you can arrange furniture around strategically positioned rugs to create different zones. Upstairs the bedrooms have more luxurious carpets for that warm-under-foot comfort that I think is vital in a country house, especially in the chillier seasons.

The biggest challenge was how to create the right atmosphere in the heart of the house: the large, double-height drawing room which is often the appealing feature of a barn conversion. I have decorated galleried rooms before, but never lived with one. Ours features an open staircase that takes you to an upper galleried level. This leads to the guest bedrooms and visually adds an element of charm and intrigue to the lofty space. Most of this living space enjoys airy headroom that extends up to the rafters. Normally you associate that sort of grand-scale height with the hall of an institutional building, so to prevent the room feeling too cold or formal, I worked hard to create different personal activity zones.

Right: *Everyone loves sitting in front of the big, open fireplace with its large club fender.*
Far right: *Fresh and neutral: I painted the plaster between the flint, brick and wooden beams in buttermilk tones and added pairs of mounted antlers in a nod to country lifestyle.*
Overleaf: *The complexity of tones in the brickwork add warmth and happily absorb strong colours such as the blue cut-velvet sofa and chairs.*

Left: *I wanted to make use of the authentic features of the barn as part of our family lifestyle. We put a flat surface across the top of the ancient hayrack to use as an area for display.*

Above: *I like to use coloured glass to mark the change of seasons in table settings. Here, different colours of harlequin glass create warm tones for winter.*

The decorative shell was dictated by the architecture. The flint and brick walls were a ready-made, lovely organic lumpy background. Paint was the only option to freshen the plaster between the flint, brick and wooden beams; I kept it fresh and neutral with an easy, buttermilk colour. Windows are uniformly dressed in simple, cream linen blinds.

Space planning was inspired by how we tend to chill out as family and like-minded friends. A wall's length of the galleried corridor above provides a relaxed, low-ceilinged area immediately in front of the big open fire. We put in possibly the largest club fender ever made to form a seating area around the fireplace – perfect for perching on and chatting with a mug of tea or a glass of wine. Comfortable sofas and two man-sized armchairs are naturally arranged around the inglenook. There is a card table, an armchair in a quiet corner, a writing desk – plenty of small areas where you can play chess or do a jigsaw or snuggle up in front of the fire with a book. The configuration makes it a place to sit and quietly read the papers, even while a group of teenagers have settled into a vicious and all-consuming board game such as Risk. It works incredibly well as a communal space and we can invite up to thirty or forty people around for a drink without it feeling at all crowded.

The complexity of tones in the wonderful brickwork projects warmth and, as a background, it can happily absorb strong colours in soft furnishings. The fabric used to re-upholster a small prayer chair (bought by my daughter for forty-five pounds at a Christie's sale) holds the entire decorative scheme of this room together. I like to mix things up – colours, patterns and textures. If you saw them merely as swatches on a mood board, you might puzzle over the combination of bold red-and-green striped linen, knockout red damask and strong, blue, jumbo corduroy which covers the sofas and chairs, but the elegant print on the prayer chair makes sense of all the solid blocks of colour in the room. It is a beautiful replication of Jacobean embroidery in myriad rich tones: red, peacock blue, teal, green and gold. A few cushions in the same fabric emphasise that touchstone palette.

A Bessarabian rug or carpet is another colour-merging ally. Bessarabian is the name commonly given to highly decorative needlepoint or tapestry-style rugs made in the late nineteenth to early twentieth century in the Russian provinces,

Far left, above left and below left: *A sense of being deep in a country location is found in every room, from the floral touches such as neo-geometric print by Claremont on the chaise longue in the master bedroom and the soft-blue rose wallpaper in the main bathroom and the Huntings Scenes wallpaper by Lewis & Wood in the downstairs cloakroom.*
Overleaf: *Hints of blue skies and gardens in bloom: I dressed the beds in faded vintage floral bedcovers and adorned the walls with botanical prints.*

imitating the woven style of the Savonnerie factory in France. They took the floral motifs of the Savonnerie technique and worked backwards, incorporating wonderful colours within a black or brown background. I often use them under a coffee or dining table, or in an upstairs hall or corridor that needs an injection of warmth and colour.

Much of the emotional character in this room comes from the disparate collection of art and objects that my husband and I have collected at different stages of our lives. Over the years we have acquired an eclectic mix of antique furniture; mostly plain strong Georgian pieces, such as the pedestal table, the red chair, and the George IV chairs that surround the card table. These work well to offset the more intricate decorative items we have amassed from our travels: a lacquer box from Burma, a Kashmiri shawl from India, my husband's skins and trophies from Africa – all merge happily with the English cottage style. In my view, good taste is simply the way in which you can give an eye-pleasing coherence to a collection of eclectic things.

Throughout the downstairs space there are also plenty of nods to the country lifestyle. This is most dramatic in the downstairs cloakroom, where I have hung Hunting Scenes wallpaper by Lewis & Wood with a matching fabric blind to make an amusing statement. Elsewhere there are pairs of mounted antlers on the wall; stuffed birds in a taxidermist's glass box; horses and dogs in the form of paintings, sculptures, ornaments and images printed on cushions; plus some ornamental wooden ducks. Woven baskets and wicker hampers stacked prettily in decreasing sizes double up as useful storage and natural decorative touches. A bowl of scented dried oranges and a grouping of fruit-shaped candles make further subtle organic flourishes.

Left: An eclectic mix of strong Georgian pieces of furniture, a lacquer table and a variety of decorative objects add emotional character to the drawing room.
Above: Rugs incorporating wonderful colours are a good way to inject warmth, as here in my daughter's pretty pastel bedroom.
Right: The upper galleried level, which leads to the guest bedrooms, adds visual charm to the lofty double-height space.

Left: *As a great believer of beauty in functionality, I do love a boot room. Hooks and shelves can be complemented by furniture that offers storage as well as decoration.*
Above: *A variety of floral touches create a serene corner of the master bedroom.*

Where possible, I have made use of authentic features so that our usage of the barn as a family house feels like part of its natural evolution. The sitting room, for example, still had its original wooden tethering posts, complete with the metal rings for the livestock's rope leads. I built a seating area between two posts to form an upholstered bench seat and filled in another section between posts to create a drinks table. Also, the kitchen/dining area retains the stone troughs and straw bale holders used for centuries by livestock. We put a flat surface across the top of the hayrack to turn the feature into a display area and kept the long, empty trough with its metal-bar dividers to use as quirky storage space.

Part of the appeal of a barn conversion is the simple way of life it promotes. A barn is all about two-room living. Everything functions in those big opened-up spaces: the sitting room and the kitchen/dining area. The kitchen is the hub of any home, and I designed it so that I can happily cook, chat and entertain simultaneously. The work surface has a raised side so that the business side of kitchen activity and its paraphernalia (chopping boards, storage jars, mixing bowls, etc.) is slightly screened from the view of those enjoying hospitality on the other side.

I plumped for a green colour scheme for the kitchen and dining area which seems fitting for the country. I personally think it is also one of the best colours to complement dark wooden furniture and colourful, pretty china. The kitchen table and dresser are painted in gentle Lulworth Blue by Farrow & Ball; a spikier, grass-green element comes in with a pair of cheery lamp bases and the green-hued glass tableware and embroidered mats I use to dress the solid, antique French table, made from oak and slate inserts.

You are so much more attuned to the seasons in the country and I like to reflect that by changing tabletops (napkins and china) and bedspreads (winter fur loses out to crisp white piqué in summer) to mark the change of seasons. The focus of living moves outside to horses, dogs and lunches in the garden. Having said that, I often have a great fire roaring in mid-August because I love the atmosphere it creates.

Upstairs, the rest of the house is made up of bedrooms and bathrooms. For paintwork I continued with country creams and added soft blues in most rooms, with a pretty floral wallpaper in the same palette in the main bathroom. Beds are dressed with faded, vintage, floral bedcovers and the walls are decorated with a framed tapestry sampler or matching botany prints. I wanted to bring a sense of the country location into every room, from the chair with the woven-rush seat in the bathroom to the eye-catching, neo-geometric floral print by Claremont on a modern chaise longue.

Above and right: Pale blue-green painted furniture, fitting for a country kitchen, is also one of the best background colours to show off pretty china.

TIPS
- See beauty in practicality. Logs stacked neatly to fill an exposed brick alcove in a country sitting room give both aesthetic pleasure and a satisfying sense of home organisation.
- Use rugs and kilims to delineate smaller, intimate areas within a large room, such as the seating arrangement in front of a fire or a space filled by a card table and chairs.
- Look to your favourite items as inspiration for a bold colour scheme. The smallest item, such as a piece of fabric, a painting or a cushion, can provide a touchstone palette.
- Make your own mood board. Pin on bits of fabric, wallpaper, colours and textures you like. Take photographs and check it is going to work on a larger scale.

KNIGHTSBRIDGE PENTHOUSE

The word 'penthouse' originally referred to a shed with a sloping roof that covered machinery on the top of a building or block of flats. Today a penthouse is synonymous with luxury rooftop living – enjoying fabulous light and eyrie-like privacy – largely thanks to the construction boom in New York City in the 1920s when economic growth prompted high demand for city apartments, and rooftops with views offered the most desirable locations.

The most famous was the publisher Condé Nast's astonishing duplex at 1040 Park Avenue, which had ten entertaining rooms on the roof, including a ballroom and a plant-filled conservatory plus a suite of sleeping and domestic rooms on the floor below. As an interior design novelty and a nexus for café society, it set a template for penthouse style.

This hip Knightsbridge penthouse may be much smaller in scale but its location fits the bill, overlooking Hyde Park from the front and boasting distinctive Brompton Road views from the rear. My clients, a young couple who emphasised how much they like to entertain, wanted to open up the living space into a big, open-plan scheme with views all the way from front to back. The apartment was characterless and modern, built to plan on two floors, but it had enormous potential to be a beautiful, light-filled space. With its generously proportioned outdoor terrace, I could see immediately how I could create 'room' spaces outside to extend the entertaining space further.

The blank canvas was actually a maze of little, boxy rooms with huge amounts of space wasted in corridors. Living according to the original floor plan would be like playing hide and seek in a labyrinth of walls and doors. The first step was to take out the bulk of the internal walls to open up latitude and perspective.

A scene-setting dramatic entrance hall is one of my trademark design features and I enjoyed the challenge of transforming the entrance area of the open-plan scheme here. The front door is situated in the centre of the floor plan and you come upstairs into an airy space with light flooding in at will, courtesy of wonderful art-glass screens. Instead of that shoulder-hunching feeling of enclosure you expect of a typical, tight apartment lobby, here you immediately feel uplifted. This is due to the lightness afforded by gorgeous sliding glass doors, which I commissioned from Polish artist, Jacek Leszczewicz.

Previous: *Led by the artwork, this eye-pleasing corner in the L-shaped drawing room achieves its harmony from a play on geometric form in the shapes of the lamp, vase and spiky plant leaves.*
Far left and left: *A vibrant 1960s-inspired flower power wallpaper creates a unity of space and pizzazz throughout the stairs, lobby and dining room. Its gold metallic background reflects light from the amazing spun-glass chandelier and the glass and mirrored furniture.*

There is a wonderful tradition of creativity and innovation in Czech and Polish glassware, to which Jacek remained true in creating an appealing, natural effect to liven up and soften the urban residential format, using leaf, twig, forest and flower motifs, which appear fossilised in the glass. The doors are particularly beautiful.

I used a very strong 1960s-inspired flower power wallpaper through the stairs, lobby and dining room, quite literally swathing the area to create spaciousness and pizzazz. It is young, fun and vivacious. The paper's gold metallic background reflects light from all angles and warm tones bounce off the rich, dark walnut floor we used throughout the entire living area to unify the space. Further sparkle comes courtesy of a mirrored chest. I love using mirrored furniture in halls. A console table or small chest of drawers can multitask as a stylish surface and an illumination-enhancer. With a great variety available on the market at affordable prices, mirrored pieces provide a good solution to a dark corner for all budgets.

Arriving up the stairs, you come through the front door into the middle of the penthouse in front of the dining room – a study in perspicacity which tantalises through Jacek's screens. I designed with a young cosmopolitan dinner party in mind.

The table, by Tim Gosling, is a wonderful statement piece with a thick clear-glass tapered surface on top of burr walnut pedestals. The tabletop rests on studs so that it appears to float. This extra visibility also celebrates the remarkable exquisiteness of the burr veneer. It's a beautiful object on its own or covered, ready to entertain. I had fun adding the funky dining chairs, which are also a statement in themselves. Upholstered in faux crocodile skin, their unusual shape and exaggerated, oval backs lend a smart, futuristic air while their colour palette of silver, ebony and cream complements the wallpaper.

Hanging beguilingly above the table as eye candy is an amazing chandelier by Sharon Marston. Wrought from hand-blown glass, it looks like a delicious tangle of fine-spun sugar. From a rectangular metallic base, a torrent of filaments tipped by florets of clear, gold and bronze-hued glass cascade down in different lengths. At the end of each filament, fibre-optics create an explosion of light and texture within the delicate hand-blown glass shapes and the metallic base shimmers when it moves in the breeze. Light bounces magically off the tabletop, windows and glass screens.

The adjoining open-plan kitchen and laid-back sitting room encapsulate the dynamic of ultra-luxe modern city living.

Above: *A contemporary hole-in-the-wall fireplace and casual shelf seating provide a focal point in the laid-back open-plan sitting area.*
Right: *The dining room is a study in perspicacity with a thick clear-glass statement table which 'floats' on burr walnut pedestals, designed by Tim Gosling.*

Left: *Note the mirrored wall solution used here, with red hand-blown lamps as art, to disguise a section of masonry that threatened to hinder the space plan.*

Continuing with the metallic-and-neutral colour scheme, the aluminium kitchen – fitted out with black granite tops and matt silver fittings – doubles up as a glamorous entertainment space with a floating glass bar seating area, beautifully lit from above. We positioned a line of three stools in black leather along the bar, coolly creating the sense that this kitchen is more about eating a takeaway from Zuma or sipping a cocktail with friends than labouring over a hot cooker.

In the sitting area, my plan incorporated the ultimate in contemporary hole-in-the-wall gas 'pebble' fires to add a warm focal point, in tune with the metropolitan environment. A deep, chunky limestone shelf runs low along the broad chimney breast. I wanted to create a comfortable, casual sitting area scattered with cushions where people can perch with a glass of wine by a fire at the end of a day – as you do in a ski chalet. With the sitting shelf, a capacious black leather ottoman, armchairs and a generous L-shaped sofa, I have catered for lots of extra perching space. This is the room where my clients

sit to enjoy their surround sound television or chill out with a movie. To inject a bit of extra cosiness, we built bookcases on either side of the chimney section and commissioned art to bring in colour. In this way the bare bones of the gentle colour palette are fleshed out with strong accent colours: blue, egg-yolk yellow, red – a contemporary mix. The bold lines of the desk, which sits in the window bay of the sitting room, are consistent with the contemporary furniture used throughout.

The drawing room on the other side of the apartment required creative thinking. The space was potentially hindered by a section of masonry that we could not remove. The solution was to mirror it in right angles on both sides and 'disguise' one side as a working cocktail cabinet; on the other side we hung stunning, red hand-blown glass lights by Dominic Phillips, to give the feeling of space and intrigue. If in doubt, use attractive lighting as an art feature.

In fact, 'lighting as art' is an integral feature of this apartment. The lighting plan throughout is designed by Sally Storey and very sophisticated in its detail and subtlety. For example, the corner opposite the cocktail cabinet in the drawing room would otherwise have been dead space had we not conjured a subtle yet dramatic experimental effect by texturing the walls with pearl plaster, literally setting crushed-up mother of pearl into a wall surface with a similar hue. This

Above and right: *We collaborated with Stephen Woodhams to differentiate the dining area from the seating area on the vast terrace using teak decking and stone as contrasts. Oversized black and cream pots and ambient lighting further delineate the mood of each space.*

was then lit very beautifully by Sally with tiny pinpoints of light to give it life as an art piece which does not compete with or detract from the focal point paintings in the drawing room. Considering the price per square foot of desirable luxury properties, you do not want to waste the potential of a single square foot of wall to add atmosphere and ambience to the overall scheme.

The troublesome masonry also gave rise to a design challenge with the floor covering in the drawing room. We installed one giant L-shaped cream rug to unify the slightly awkward spaces, but I cannot tell you how difficult it was to calculate the exact corner point!

All the colour on top of the neutral scheme has been created with art, objects and clever lighting. For this space I commissioned a triptych by Hugh Fairfax, inspired by the light, flat and eternal seascape of the Norfolk coast. His contemporary use of muted bold colour contributes to the personality of the room. When it comes to building up a 'look' around a neutral palette, you have to play with the weight of the layering – and go cautiously. That is not just a question of assessing the right amount of texture or pattern, but colour too. It is a question of knowing when to stop. You can always add, but it is hard to take elements away.

I particularly like the way this drawing room corner has worked so prettily [see picture]. Look closely, and you will see a lot of emphasis on putting together different shapes to complement the play on geometric forms in the two pictures: the wacky proportions of the lamp, the long spiky plant leaves, the sumptuously curved arms of the chair and sofa corners. It all adds up to a thoroughly eye-pleasing, L-shaped spot.

Terraces can often be narrow, but the outdoor roof space here is fabulous – so big that it easily accommodates more than a hundred friends for a party. I worked on designing the outdoor sitting and dining areas with Stephen Woodhams. We put teak decking under the dining room part of the terrace; in contrast, we positioned the seating area, with its low table for candles and drinks, on top of stone. Oversized black and cream pots, big trees and moody lighting further delineate the lovely different spaces and ambience. Beyond the areas designed for particular use, there is still plenty of room to relax in. The client asked us to incorporate a collection of appealing glass fish so we designed this low, bubbling fountain, whereby the fish are part swimming and part flying above the water level. High up, with wonderful views and a sense of eyrie-like privacy, this terrace is particularly rewarding as an example of outdoors/indoors design. All you need is good weather!

The living space is for 'public' consumption, but in an apartment of this size the private rooms – bedrooms, dressing room, bathroom – must also share the same overall look and feel of the design scheme. To achieve a master bedroom complete with waft into his-and-hers dressing rooms, we took out a couple of walls, but added a distinct architectural feel with a contemporary four-poster bed made of nickel, with mirrored panels and a polished walnut finish. It picks up some of the design motifs – the mirroring and walnut – and it is quite a design statement in its own right, with strong boxy lines.

The rest of the room is very fresh and gentle with simple ivory walls, cream lacquer furniture and layers of shimmering curtains. The spectacular effect of the curtains is due to the fabric - a wonderful Neisha Crosland satin concoction where the pattern has been burnt out to create the textured design. This sheer layer is the feature of the window dressing, and underneath it lies the more utilitarian light-blocking cotton/linen lining layer – not sewn in - for use at night. It's the reverse of having voile curtains on inside.

The reverse side of the wall behind the bed is actually a mirrored screen dividing the bedroom from the bathroom and dressing-rooms, and allowing space for a dressing table with cupboards on the opposite wall. Throughout the flat, knobs on doors and pieces of furniture – as in the nut shells on the bedside chests here – reflect the organic leaves and reeds in the central glass-art screens.

In addition to the curtains, further softness in the room comes from the matching bloom paintings on either side of the bed and a sculpture, celebrating the curves of a female torso, which sits on a glass pedestal. The Realist painting from Plus One Gallery inspire the colour accents in the room, notably grass green and apple red. Cushions have a red trim around a green square centre; elsewhere vibrant green comes in glassware. The bedroom is equipped for a modern lifestyle: a television rises up out of a chest of drawers at the press of a button. It's a key luxurious touch now to have a television in the bedroom, but also good to be able to hide it. Increasingly we are building reading lights into bed posts, and keeping the bedside light as a more decorative lamp. It's so practical if you don't want to disturb your partner with your book or kindle.

There is room on the floor plan, too, for a guest bedroom – continuing the young, metallic theme with a glorious sunburst mirror above the bed - and bathroom, as well as a house office-cum-walk-in store for the washing machines and ironing board. The modern design of apartment blocks often provide useful storage underground close to the parking zone, but when you've opted for an open-plan designer kitchen, you will always have some domestic clutter to put away and keep out of sight.

Left and above: The outdoor terrace boasts wonderful views and eyrie-like privacy. The space can accommodate more than 100 friends for a party; for additional eye-candy, we incorporated my client's collection of glass fish into the design of a low, bubbling fountain.

TIPS

- Mirrored furniture is a useful means of brightening a dark or dingy corner. It can look absolutely stunning, it is affordable and it is not hard to find on the high street.
- Use beautiful lighting to create interest while preserving a sense of spaciousness in a room. Adopt the motto 'lighting as art'!
- Build reading lights into bedposts and keep lighting on bedside tables purely decorative. This is not only a practical and selfless way of reading at night without disturbing your partner, but also means you can pick out pretty bedside lamps without worrying about wattage or the angle of the light source.
- Think of outdoor space and gardens as extra entertaining rooms, which can often work well as an extension of the indoor design statement. Delineate dining/relaxing space with trees in pots and different types of flooring.

Previous: *Layers of shimmering, sheer curtains keep the ivory palette fresh and gentle, led by a wonderful textured satin fabric designed by Neisha Crosland.*
Left: *The contemporary four-poster bed made of nickel and polished walnut takes the design motifs of the living space into the master bedroom.*
Below: *The private rooms of an apartment must share the clean design lines of the public living space, as exemplified in this upstairs bathroom.*

DONNE
HOUSE

My trademark decorative style is to add colour, texture and pattern onto a neutral shell to create layers of comfort, so it was particularly memorable for me when, working in the opposite direction to layering up, I felt the thrill an archaeologist must experience when hitting upon treasure.

This euphoria of discovery occurred in a Victorian house with Edwardian additions in Cambridge, which my clients had bought from someone who had been forced to abandon it mid-restoration. The house had originally been built in 1880 at the cost of £463, and it is a perfect example of Victorian Gothic 'Lite'. The approach through the gate and up the drive is exactly the same as it would have been when it was built. You enter a world redolent of dons, academia and serious endeavour. My brief was to complete the restoration upgrade and period repairs, as well as to redo the joinery and decorate the non-historic areas of the house from scratch.

We were peeling off some horrible blue paisley-patterned paper from the walls in the dining room when in-between the picture rail and the cornice, we happened upon an incredible classical frieze. The great joy was that this long stretch of decoration extended all the way around the room, albeit in various stages of repair. Most clients would want something brand spanking new but the house's owners have an intelligent and sympathetic appreciation of period detail, as well as a profound interest in the classical world, so they loved the notion of historic fragments. We simply cleaned the frieze, undertook some touching up and were able to safeguard about sixty to seventy per cent of it, regarding it as complete. On the wall underneath we hung a warm sun-on-wheat-field coloured silk and trimmed the frieze top and bottom with gilt edging – the effect is wonderful. It creates a distinctive talking point for dining room company.

The original decoration in the dining room was inspired by the peacock blue in the strong and colourful geometric pattern in the historic Watts paper used in the grand Puginesque entrance hall and staircase. You have to be careful with Victorian Gothic. A smidgeon too much and the overall look is over the top, in my opinion. Once we had removed the blanket of blue paper, the gorgeous Rubelli silk weave curtains came into their own, with the sophisticated floral motifs seeming to float on the iridescent silk in the changing light.

Previous: *The grand Puginesque hall – complete with timber-vaulted roof, sturdy staircase and original Gothic lantern – gives the house a strong historic footprint. The peacock blue in the historic Watts paper led the colour palette in our refurbishment throughout the house.*
Far left: *We leavened the Victorian 'dark hall' genre by respecting the tradition but finding contemporary brightness in the use of fresh white paint and simple furnishings.*
Left: *Witty near-symmetry: two Dutch gables feature on the façade which is a play on high Victorian architecture.*

Left and below: *In the process of peeling off old wallpaper in the dining room, we discovered a classical frieze in various states of repair. Cleaned and trimmed with gilt it creates a distinctive talking point. We also lucked upon the perfect mid-Victorian oak dining table and matching arch-backed chairs at Bonhams.*

As we were in the process of putting together a considerable antique collection for the clients, we were very much attuned to saleroom stock. At Bonhams we immediately lucked upon a wonderful mid-Victorian brown and pollard oak banded dining table, as well as sixteen matching chairs with solid arched padded backs. They are classic Pugin oak pieces. We then spent the next year looking for a complementary serving table to fit in the alcove next to the fireplace. In the meantime, we sourced a glamorous sideboard cabinet which fitted precisely along the other available wall space, complete with elegant brass-grille doors, backed by pleated silk and pilaster details. To balance out the Victoriana for contemporary taste, I chose to hang an antique Baccarat crystal chandelier which beautifully offsets the Persian carpet and oak furniture with its delicate and crisp play of light. We also could not resist acquiring a Victorian crystal tazza (a shallow, saucer-like dish for holding fruits, sweets or nuts) mounted on an ormolu base showcasing figures in classical poses, to use as a focal point in the middle of the table or on the sideboard.

With its two Dutch gables, the property has a grand symmetrical facade – the very epitome of the high Victorian taste that became popular after Pugin designed the Houses of Parliament in Gothic style in the late 1830s. Set back between two handsome, red-brick bay windows, the big wooden double

doors meet in the middle to form an arch shape. The door, approached by three low steps, is set within a vaulted portico with ornamental stone embellishments. The formal entrance would have a slightly institutional air were it not for the fact that you walk first into a draught lobby and then into the Gothic hall, where light floods in from four doors opening out into fresh and bright rooms. It would have been easy to go for Arts and Crafts on the inside, but I find that look uncomfortable and we specialise in comfort. The sturdy staircase, lofty timber-vaulted roof and densely patterned wallpaper were true to the Victorian dark hall genre, but we worked hard to respect the tradition within a simpler, airier environment. We cleaned the timber vaulting; stained, polished and cleaned the floors; and spruced up the Gothic lantern which had been made for the house in the late nineteenth century.

The contemporary brightness comes from keeping things clean and fresh in white eggshell, including the banisters, the underside of the staircase landings, the upstairs hall door arches, skirting boards and draught hall doors. The draught hall and alcoves boasted the original Victorian tiles – pattern layered on pattern, colour on colour – but I chose to highlight

Left: *Easy-living vibe: fresh white walls and a Moleanos limestone floor in the Orangery maximise the natural light that floods in through the slanted glass roof and floor-to-ceiling windows. The blue and yellow colour accents are reflected in the painting American White Pelican by Audubon.*
Below: *Antique school cloakroom hooks and oak shoe locker benches add to the heritage feel of the boot room.*

sections of it and keep furnishings to the centre because the perimeter surroundings are already so dramatic. The hall is furnished with a single, late Regency, circular rosewood table sitting on a pretty Persian carpet which sympathetically picks up the colours of the wallpaper.

A house with a strong historic footprint is rewarding to refit and update. The professor's library, for example, was just waiting to be fitted out as a classic gentleman's mahogany library. We bought the stately Regency bookcase with its wonderful inlay detailing and glazed doors at auction, and built the rest of the library around it to match in tone and colour. We installed period reading lights above both sides of a squashy leather chesterfield. The fireplace was accessorised with a sturdy club fender and a don-and-pupil set of facing armchairs. A lovely, nubbly grass cloth in a fawn colour on the walls gives a solid, masculine feel. Texture on the walls creates a more comfortable shell for a home study than paint; it also makes an excellent background to show off a painting or to unite a mix of paintings. A pair of oversized antique obelisks layered in specimen marble stand on the mantelpiece. A contrast-trimmed loop wool rug on the wooden floor adds a further contemporary touch.

The library leads into the working quarter of the house, with a further home office and book room for storage of academic volumes, filing, photos and so on. We had fun enlivening the guest cloakroom with a toile de Jouy wallpaper featuring classical Roman architectural scenes; this is complemented by a black marble surround for the basin, dark wood cabinetry and shelves displaying classic vases, bowls and boxes.

You do not immediately notice unless you study the facade, but the left-hand side of the house – which looks out over a pretty garden with a parterre and mature trees – is deeper and taller than the other elevation. It is taller by virtue of the twist of the staircase rising up half a landing (giving extra height to the ground floor drawing and dining rooms) and deeper because it comprises the original drawing and dining rooms; it also has a wonderful orangery-style conservatory and a large boot room opening out onto the garden. The back section was added later. Original plans of the house show it was drafted as a small conservatory with a corridor running alongside and walk-in cupboards to house boots, knives, a loo and the gun room. Today that original layout has become one large vibrant space with a modern feel.

Left: *The drawing room represents a lovely versatile entertaining space with different seating group areas furnished in an appealing mix of antique and new items. Armchairs upholstered in the distinctive peacock blue in the hall frame the fireplace as a focal point. Note the visual trick in the semi-unfolded Roman blind which covers several feet of wall above a regular glass door.*
Overleaf: *Note the individually sourced antique lights in the drawing room here, and throughout the property, often created by converting decorative objects into occasional lamps.*

Above: *A classic gentleman's mahogany library with period reading lights and a fireplace accessorised with a sturdy club fender and a don-and-pupil set of armchairs.*
Right: *An immaculately detailed Georgian secretaire, in satinwood, mahogany and sycamore, adds elegance and gravitas to a corner of the drawing room.*

The drawing room is a clever mix of antique and new furniture. My clients had a refreshingly open mind about mixing and reworking items. We scoured the salesrooms on their behalf – a fantastic way to buy furniture. I have a close relationship with Bonhams, Sotheby's and Christie's. We keep tabs on the provincial salerooms too and receive updated information via subscription and catalogues. I advise never to be afraid of buying something a bit worn or beaten up; in Britain we have access to marvellous restorers and highly skilled specialists who can repaint, re-gild, re-mould, re-upholster – you name it. The prize piece in the drawing room, however, needed no work. It is an immaculate Georgian secretaire in satinwood, mahogany and sycamore. In its corner position, it adds elegance and a quiet gravitas with its pull-down writing drawer revealing a tooled leather surface and an interior fitted with tiny drawers and pigeonholes.

You come into the drawing room from the hall, drawn by the light and pretty colour palette; warm tones of cream, gold and coral with that distinctive peacock blue from the Gothic wallpaper, again picked out in the border of the rug, in the fabric on the two fireside armchairs and in paler hues on the curtain trimming and velvet cushions. This is a lovely, versatile entertaining space. We designed for several seating groups within the room to cater for small or large parties. There is a pairing of chairs either side of a buttoned ottoman in front of the fireplace, which faces the main sofa and armchair combination arranged around the glass coffee table. For an alternative seating scenario, we also positioned two upright chairs around a black and gold lacquer coffee table, opposite the cushioned seating in the bay window. The warm heart to the room is created by a lovely rug, handmade in France by Ateliers Pinton, with a geometric pattern cut into an understated two-tone neutral palette.

Please note the specially sourced antique lights. The client wanted every single light fitting in the house (except downlighters in the practical 'below stairs' areas) to be antique. It was extremely hard work to source the right decorative objects to convert into occasional lamps, but the result is beautiful. The lamps are as much pieces of art as they are practical lights.

Solid, white-painted double doors lead into the dining room, which can also be accessed from the hall. A glass door, heightened by a horizontal pane of glass above it, leads into the light and airy orangery. Fresh white walls and a Moleanos limestone floor maximise the natural light that

floods in through the slanted glass roof and floor-to-ceiling glass windows. The vibe here is all about more informal living – comfy L-shaped seating and no antique wood surfaces to protect. We found an attractive armoire to house crockery and a sympathetic contemporary dining table which is accessorised with a set of curved-back wooden chairs, upholstered in fun blue, yellow, green and white stripes. We were thrilled to find the traditional, marble-topped French baker's table: its black wrought iron support beautifully complements the black iron roof supports. The blue and yellow accented colour scheme is led by the painting American White Pelican by Audubon, who was famous for being the first ornithologist-painter to depict birds in their natural habitat. We picked up on the blue again in the paisley-patterned, L-shaped sofa, the Chinese porcelain, the cushions and the tableware.

At the rear is a serious boot room. It is a luxury in itself to have a spacious room like this with practical storage, a ceramic basin and counter to arrange cut flowers, plus tiled floor space to deal with all the clobber and clothing that come with outdoor life. We installed antique school cloakroom hooks and a shoe locker bench and built in joinery in antiqued oak to match. Rows of small, mounted antlers add a heritage feel to this, the newest part of the house. I have mentioned before how I equally enjoy designing and fitting out the practical rooms in

Below: *Tartan wool is used to create a masculine effect in an attic bedroom.*
Right: *The primary guest bedroom is a good example of the spirit of reworking the best of the original fittings. We salvaged the creamy gold silk curtains from the original drawing room and reused them for the outer layer of bed curtains. The overall calm aura is enhanced by layers of silk-on-silk sheen and the lustre of the antique porcelain lamp bases and vases that sit on top of the wardrobe.*

Left: *The master bedroom features a bespoke four-poster bed made in 19th-century style but with 21st-century proportions and comfort, and dressed to a 'no-frills, clean lines' brief in a gorgeous Bennison hand-printed linen.*
Below: *The classical-themed Toile du Jouy wallpaper and mirror with frieze in the downstairs cloakroom combine to provide a witty nod to the classical theme.*

the house as well as the 'public' living and entertaining spaces. I feel I have truly done my job well when I allocate a space for an ironing board. Well, here I was in heaven as we transformed a dank, dark basement – which the original plans show to have been marked for Beer, Wine, and Rolling Way for Heating Charcoal – into a fabulous laundry room and wine cellar.

The layout on the first floor provides for four large double bedrooms, each with its own bathroom, plus a dressing room apiece for my clients. We built in rather stately mahogany wardrobe storage in 'his' dressing room, which doubles up as an upstairs sitting-room en suite to the master bedroom. There are two further guest bedrooms on the second floor, both maintaining lovely proportions.

The primary guest bedroom, which comes off the grand galleried staircase, is a good example of the principle of metamorphosis at work behind our overall scheme. We salvaged the gold and cream silk curtains from the original drawing room and transformed them into curtains with pelmets. We also reused the fabric for the outer layer of bed curtains, which drape from the coronet and enclose a gathered blue silk lining. However, what pulls this room together are the framed panels of Chinoiserie that hang on either side of the fireplace, resonating with warm gold colours and delicate birds and foliage. Like our dining room revelation, we were thrilled to find these panels in the process of stripping back the drawing room and we were determined to move them elsewhere in the spirit of reworking the best of the original fittings. The overall aura is calm and restful, enhanced by layers of silk-on-silk sheen and the lustre of the antique celadon crackle porcelain lamp bases and dove-grey ornamental vases that sit on top of the wardrobe. The walls are a gentle aqua blue, a shade we have picked up with cream in the needlepoint rug, in the stunning silk pleated lining of the bed hangings and in the fabric on the low wingback sofa at the end of the bed.

Left: *The discreet in-built mahogany wardrobe storage enables this room to double up as both 'his' dressing room and an upstairs sitting-room en suite to the master bedroom.*

TIPS

- Explore the salerooms. You will be surprised at the variety and affordability of furniture. Do not be afraid if an item is a bit battered; you can achieve a lot with re-upholstery, repainting or a good polish. Remember, we are a nation of specialist craftspeople.
- A house that has evolved in its decorative scheme is often more intimate than a property with a complete refit. Look for old features to celebrate. Frame sections of original curtain fabric, tapestry or wallpaper and hang as art. Recycle downstairs curtains, moving them up to bedrooms.
- For a truly individual touch, it is gratifyingly simple to convert your favourite vases, urns or wide-bottomed bottles into pretty lamp bases. A pair of small chests of drawers on either side of the bed usefully doubles up as bedside tables and extra storage.

The client wanted a traditional four-poster bed to be the main feature of the master bedroom, but one without frills. I do not recommend buying an antique four-poster at auction unless you are less than five foot tall and not interested in king-size width, boxed springs and quality mattresses. The average height of a man was a good four or five inches less in the eighteenth and nineteenth centuries than it is today. We had this bed frame made in early nineteenth-century style but of twenty-first-century proportions, and dressed it with neat lines in a gorgeous, Bennison hand-printed linen. The palette of crisp sky blue and creams, highlighted by orange and buttercup yellow, inspired the rest of the soft furnishings. Again, we found some lovely elegant antique pieces: the long stool at the foot of the bed, the matching pair of chests of drawers, used as bedside tables, and the chaise longue – another subtle nod to the classical theme. I have to say I think this pair of bedside lamps is the most beautiful I have ever seen; the delicate and intricate shape plus the lightness of the Chinese porcelain vases on ormolu mounts make these special objets d'art.

Right: *The framed panels of hand-painted Chinoiserie silk that hang either side of the fireplace in the guest bedroom are a good example of the spirit of metamorphosis behind our redecoration scheme. We discovered the panels when stripping back the drawing room and determined to use them elsewhere in the house. See also page 135.*

LE
LIRADOU

Some houses stand out as a unique feature in their landscape; some owe their charm to being an organic part of their surroundings. Le Liradou – situated close to Grasse, in the coastal region of Provence known as the Maritime Alps – is a delightful example of the latter category, providing the ultimate in harmonious Côte d'Azur indoor/outdoor living.

From the outside, its stone walls, lavender-blue hued shutters and low, sloping roofs of rounded tiles blend beautifully into the granite 'mountainscape', fragrant fields and sun-scorched earth around. From the inside, a palette of neutrals spiked with blues, lilacs, silver-greys, creamy gold and terracotta reflects the gorgeous spring and summer season outside: olive groves shimmering beneath cerulean skies and cool, cream sunshades and cushioned, rattan sunbeds beckoning you to relax and drink in the fragrance of herbs on the warm breeze.

As well as providing a comfortable retreat from the balmy temperatures in high summer, I was brought in to help remodel the house to offer an elegant living space that works all year round, with plenty of vistas to celebrate the stunning views from every window.

The house was originally a mas, or farmstead, typical of the rural architecture of Provence. It stands in the middle of a vast olive grove, on a hillside looking out towards the Mediterranean Sea. Historically, a mas was built as a self-sufficient unit which would produce fruit, vegetables, olives, wine, meat, milk and cheese; it faced south to provide protection from the mistral. Such a house was usually constructed as a long rectangle, two or three storeys high, with the family kitchen and space for animals on the ground floor and bedrooms and further food

Previous: *Provencal paradise: the indoor/outdoor living dynamic celebrates alfresco summer living.*
Left: *A beautiful David Linley round table in blonde wood is the central feature in the open and airy hall.*
Above: *Curved ironwork extends as a railing around the gallery hall creating an air of grandeur that calls for a formal arrangement of mirror, console and paired chairs.*

storage on the first; it would have small, narrow windows to keep out the heat in summer and to retain warmth in the winter.

At first sight, I could see my client's house had a handsome basic structure but no internal character at all. It was acquired as one of those heart-sinking conversions, undertaken with the cheapest fittings and no sense of style or historical integrity. However, it did have huge potential, set in its own land with olive groves to the front and back. We set about gutting it with the assistance of local contractors, opening up the small rooms and enlarging the windows to showcase as much of the spirit-lifting views as possible: the Provençal countryside by day, the incredible stars at night.

You get a lovely sense of tranquility by establishing an easy flow between inside and outside. On this we worked in collaboration with Jean Mus, the Provençal landscape gardener who is celebrated for his poetic flourishes and passion for details. 'Gardens are a game of seduction,' he likes to say. 'They lure you into their theatre of décor.' With a respect for the view from the house's windows, he set about creating charming

vistas and quiet corners framed by trees and plants; he also provided for those all-important areas of shadow you need to protect against the sun during the three or four months of intense summer sun.

The house is approached by a hillside road coming down from behind. The front door is inset within a low-arched stone entrance and takes you into a large hall which we kept open and airy; a beautiful David Linley round table in blonde wood is the central feature. You walk into the house but you see right through it to the open-plan dining and drawing room area and beyond; your eyes are drawn in by its spectacular picture window and the perspective it frames; a vast blue sky, distant blue-grey hilltops, the narrow crowns of inky-dark Mediterranean cypress trees and pretty roses in bloom.

Throughout the ground level we put in new floors in antique limestone. To the right of the building, as you stand in the hall, is the cosy study and separate sitting room. To the left are the kitchen and pantry and the staircase. We held on to the existing, sweeping staircase, which is well proportioned and features delicate ironwork. On the first floor the curved ironwork – a great French skill – extends as a railing around the gallery hall, creating an air of mellow grandeur that allows for a series of family portraits and the formal mirror-and-console arrangement of paired chairs, lamps and wall sconces.

The drawing room is an oasis of calm comfort, soft-furnished in creams and the palest of olive-greys. In sunny seasons nothing distracts from the views through the picture window. Without any glazing bars, this large rectangle of glass creates a painting of the view. The window and the French doors are framed with neutral, pleated curtains with a gossamer-sheer inner layer hung from a simple black iron curtain pole. There is huge variance in the strength of light throughout the day in this part of the world so it is important to provide levels of shade. Furniture is traditional French to maintain the idiom. Glassware – in the form of storm lanterns, tall glass lamps and a range of jugs and decanters – contributes towards the indoor/outdoor dynamic.

Left: Absolute comfort: the sitting room has a strong seasonal feel thanks to the gorgeous ottoman covered in lavender ribbed-weave fabric.
Below: Natural stoneware and ornamental gourds in the cabinet echo the organic feel projected by the arrangement of Besler botanical prints.

In the winter, the handsome fireplace might become more of a focus than the view outside and the room must work as a more enclosed space. The natural theme is accentuated by the sturdy rush basket full of logs for the fire and the armchairs made from a fine dove-grey rattan that decorate the dining room.

The same cream walls and ceilings and the golden limestone floor tiles create a neutral shell in the little study off the drawing room. Original beams add a sense of architectural intimacy; plain linen curtains hang from a dark wood pole on leather clips. A comfy saddle-brown leather armchair and foot stool – signature pieces from Ralph Lauren – plus a trimmed sisal rug lend physical warmth while a wall lined with antique bookcases to display favourite tomes and family photographs bring in the personal touches. The bookcases, which we repainted and adapted to suit the wall, boast rarely seen original hinges and locks. An elegant Louis XVI-style armchair with classic oval cane backrest works both as a functional desk chair and as the cameo item that adds a touch of French flair in the room.

For absolute feet-up comfort in soft seating, the sitting room beckons. Again, it is an extension of the resolutely neutral shell palette, accentuated luxuriously by two cream club sofas and a coordinating armchair with footstool, arranged cosily around three walls. A gorgeous ottoman covered in a rich, lavender ribbed-weave Manuel Canovas fabric is the eye candy. Six magnificent Besler botanical prints are arranged symmetrically on the wall to add a strong seasonal feel, which is boosted by the natural stoneware, green porcelain and ornamental gourds displayed in the corner cabinet.

The sultry temperatures of high summer can make the thought of getting up to prepare lunch for family and guests a bit of an effort, but not when your kitchen is a delightfully cool and calm place in which to retreat. The kitchen here is restful and soothing but also homely, thanks to the original ceiling beams and the low arches that divide the working area and pantry from the table. The idea was to keep it simple and practical, with plenty of storage in the form of built-in refrigerators, pantry cupboards and wine racks. The shell is essentially a cocoon of warm cream – the walls, limestone floors, painted ceiling (beams and all) and built-in cabinets – which is both a cool retreat from the sun and a suitable environment for preparing the lunchtime salad Niçoise, piles of prawns, and plates of charcuterie and cheese.

Pretty blue and white checked fabrics add softening touches as blinds and chair cushions, inspired by the china and crockery stored behind the glass doors of the kitchen cupboard. As throughout, a traditional look works well here. We were not pushing boundaries in design, merely playing with what was right and appropriate in the most stylish way.

This was particularly the case in the bedrooms. The master bedroom rejoices in wonderful views from two aspects. The aim was to keep it airy and simple while injecting a fresh vibe into traditional French style. We hung a weighty Pierre Frey cream

Left: *Eyes are drawn in by the spectacular picture window in the drawing room and the perspective it frames: beautiful countryside by day, stars in an inky sky by night.*
Above, top and bottom: *Tranquil outdoor living: the distinguished Provencal landscape gardener Jean Mus created charming vistas and quiet corners.*
Overleaf: *An oasis of calm and shade, the drawing room is soft furnished in luxurious creams and the palest of olive-greys.*

fabric, richly embroidered with floral motifs, as curtains on the windows and from the coronet above the bed. We contrasted this with an oversized blue and white check on the bedhead, valance and as a trim to the characteristically Mediterranean matelassé bedspread; we added bold cushions in deep-sea blue and claret red. The bed canopy hangs from an antique coronet which we repainted and the bed itself is framed by a pair of Nicky Haslam commodes, which are a contemporary take on a Louis XV chest of drawers.

Note the semi-circular coffer in the ceiling, which we installed to add scale and movement to a large space and which runs the full length of the room, delineating different areas of the room and giving the illusion of raised ceiling height. The open cylindrical fire and ceiling coffer in the middle of the room creates a natural cosy corner in the winter or for cool, shady reading at siesta time in the summer. Arguably, the most mood-enhancing view on this floor is enjoyed from the glorious cast-iron bathtub in the huge L-shaped space that comprises the en-suite dressing and bathroom. You can imagine lying in deep lavender-scented water, with the local triple-milled soap to hand, looking out through the floor-to-ceiling window onto the garden and horizon beyond.

Left: *Traditional French dining furniture, a rustic armoire and an array of glassware maintain the indoor/outdoor idiom.*
Below: *Restful and soothing in cream, the kitchen has plenty of built-in storage. Low arches and original ceiling beams divide the working area and pantry from the table.*

We carried the bold blue and white check through onto the walls here, which is fun, and used every corner of the room to build in storage with an L-shaped 'wall feature' comprising five double-door wardrobes. The top panel section of each set of closet doors is lined with shirred gingham behind chicken wire which prettifies an otherwise solid length of joinery. We used contrasting wallpaper in vertical stripes through the back of the wardrobes and the result is ultra-glamorous. To further enhance the blue and white theme, we took an unremarkable antique cabinet and turned it into a vanity unit, repainting its trim with blue highlights.

Toile de Jouy is universally recognised as a French decorative feature: a distinctive white or off-white background on which a repeated pattern in a single colour (most often black, dark red or blue) depicts a fairly complex narrative scene. Originally it was produced as a cheap fabric with a witty pattern – often with a classical or allegorical theme – to be used as slip covers or dust sheets to protect silk and embroidered furniture or curtains from the sun. The themes became more elaborate as toiles became more popular from the late eighteenth century onwards. Toile was an obvious feature to play with here.

Below: *Checks on the wall add fun in the en-suite bathroom and dressing room. Note the double-door wardrobe joinery, prettified with shirred gingham behind chicken wire.*
Right: *The contrast between floral motifs and bold blue-and-white checks injects a fresh vibe into traditional French style in the master bedroom.*

As my client is not an advocate of fluff or clutter and has a strong pull towards colour, we were pleased to find a quirky, rich red toile on a caramel background to anchor a guest bedroom. A traditional French sleigh bed with matching bedside cabinets and complementary chest of drawers contribute to a masculine feel in this room. Dark wood is a unifying feature in the frames of the mirror and paintings, the occasional lamp base and the curtain poles. Chocolate brown, claret and toffee make up the palette for the soft furnishings.

This room also benefits from a dual aspect with a pair of narrow casements as well as the main 'big outlook' window. The comfort of a bedroom here depends on temperature and ambience of lighting, hence the layering of shutters, the sheer fabrics and curtains on the window, the large, effective fan, and the flickering candles in storm lanterns for a romantic evening.

A significant part of my brief was to decorate to enhance my client's collection of twentieth- and twenty-first-century paintings, notably work by the Scottish colourists. Their highly developed use of colour encapsulates the philosophy of our own decorative dynamic. During the 1920s and 1930s, this group of painters absorbed and reworked the strong and vibrant colours of contemporary French painting (Monet, Matisse and Cézanne) into a fresh and distinctive idiom of their own. On a domestic level, we were also taking the best visual aspects of the locality and applying it to our contemporary interior design vision.

The way we cut the colours of olive foliage and Provençal sky with a neutral background in the second guest bedroom illustrates this well. It is French in its own way, in the harmonious blend of colours, the delicate painted ironwork shelves and light sconces, the pretty painted furniture and cane-backed dressing table chair. We sourced the marble and ceramic bathroom tiles locally so that there was an organic integrity. The overall impression is modern and fresh, underpinned by a bold blue 'reverse' toile we used as fabric and wallpaper; it contrasts beautifully with the white Victorian porcelain washstand and white carved mirror frames.

Left: *A fresh take on the French idiom: a bold blue 'reverse' toile as blinds and wallpaper contrasts beautifully with the white Victorian porcelain washstand and white carved mirror frames.*

- Do source antique porcelain sanitary ware. In a period property, bathrooms often ruin a theme if kitted out with modern sinks and tubs. Vintage pieces add character and style. However, I do not recommend old taps and fittings as it is too difficult to find spare parts for the working bits.

- Look out for old chests of drawers, cupboards or commodes to repaint. Take off the top and replace it with stone or marble and you have a fabulous new piece of furniture.

- Built-in wardrobes can block out space. I like to put contrasting wallpaper on the back wall to regain a sense of depth and add a touch of glamour.

- Think seriously about the orientation of your bath and what you would most like to look at. A window? A painting? Definitely not the door!

Right: *A quirky rich red and caramel Toile de Jouy anchors the scheme of a guest bedroom.*
Overleaf: *Wicker chairs, local stone and a lavish array of glassware provide organic touches to the dream south of France alfresco summer lunch table.*

HYDE
LODGE

Your home is your castle, so the saying goes, but few contemporary luxury homes look like palaces from the outset. My particular mission in this extraordinary house in Knightsbridge was to create a masterpiece of introspective decoration. The property was originally a dull box carved from three small houses, situated in a modern environment with a commercial feel. Nestled in-between other buildings, it has no significant windows on the ground floor. Most of the natural light comes from above, which means it is bright but it has no outlook.

To say this was a difficult site is an understatement, but it is the kind of design challenge I embrace wholeheartedly. I had to conjure up internal focal points and decorate to the centre in accordance with my clients' ultra-sophisticated international taste. It was fascinating to set my mind to an alien concept; thinking inside the box.

I was given the property as a shell, so on one level it was a complete refurbishment; a glorious blank canvas, on which I would also incorporate the clients' art collection. On a more fundamental level, the challenge lay in creating a beautiful internal landscape and a sense of liberating spaciousness within the windowless walls. We had to assess the existing infrastructure and determine how best to incorporate the new design with minimal damage to the structure. Starting this unusual process of working from the outside in, we altered two utilitarian staircases to add visual stimulus and warmth; under the expert guidance of lighting expert Sanjit Bahra, we significantly upgraded the wiring and lighting throughout. It required some clever engineering and electrical solutions to bring extra cables to the space without taking down walls.

The hall is a wonderful double-height entrance room, top lit from the glass ceiling above. To add pure drama in this aerial space, I commissioned a magnificent, fine chain mail chandelier (1.2 metres in diameter and 200 kg in weight) made by the New York designer, Barlas Baylar for Terzani. Hundreds of metres of softly-draped nickel chain form an eye-catching sculpture; an elegant cascade of flowing metal. The piece adds a spectacular, shimmering presence to an airy space and fills the void magnificently. The hard tactility of the metal is offset by the gauzy, delicate effect of the gathered chains lit from within. We increasingly decorate with light in a sculptural sense as well as to provide a light source – on some occasions we even light that light source. Here we extended the radiant effect with matching

Previous: *Surreal style in the dining room: Tim Gosling cut the pedestals for the Chinoiserie urns with Perspex so they appear to float against the decorative backdrop of a dreamlike tropical rainforest wrought from ornamental plaster relief.*
Far left: *I like to use light as decorative drama. Here, the fine chain mail chandelier and matching ornamental wall brackets project a gauzy, delicate radiance in the double-height airy entrance room.*
Left: *A funky 1960s print on a chesterfield in the study adds levity in a masculine palette while a 3D canvas, covered in gold-lacquered starfish, adds an element of surprise and beauty.*

Left: *The overall aim in the study was for an ultra-sophisticated calmness, achieved by maintaining clean lines.*
Above: *The in-built joinery matches the walnut and ivory lacquer of the furniture; the audio-visual wall has been designed to resemble a sleek chimney breast.*

ornamental wall brackets. I have said before that I love to inject drama into an entrance because it stirs anticipation for what the rest of the house might be like. Subconsciously you want visitors to think, 'Wow! I wonder what happens next.' This is a perfect example of theatrical eye-candy that simultaneously provides stunning light quality from halogen bulbs concealed within an ethereally beautiful, functional work of art.

The circular table below the chandelier was made by Tim Gosling, with whom I often collaborate; the shape of the top and base echoes the rounded shape of the chandelier, as does the beautiful silk carpet it sits on. Taken in with a vertical sweep of the eye, they make a series of circles precisely placed within the square motif of the floor. This adds an extra sculptural dimension to the space design. A nickel insert around the perimeter of the rosewood and ebony table adds a subtle sympathy to the floor-to-ceiling look, and the faceted mirror sections around the side of the tabletop strongly complement the play of light from above. Note the ripple in the integral spiral pattern of the rug, hand-shaven to suggest the rays of light project from the facets of the mirror. The soft, dramatic lighting is further enlivened by the way it bounces off walls finished in stucco Veneziano

(the sixteenth-century Italian tradition of polishing pre-tinted plaster to a marble-like lustre), the mirrored panels around the rich wood front door and the glass-sided staircase etched with motifs and decorative effects in gold leaf.

The long, rectangular drawing room luxuriates in a one-and-a-half height ceiling, but as a shell, its lack of eye-level windows and its rectangular shape gave it a potentially claustrophobic, industrial atmosphere. My first step was to remove a functional staircase and replace it with a softer, more aesthetically appealing series of floating steps that turn a corner and lead up to the study. As structural alterations go, it was a small one, but it readily removed the 'boxiness' of the original layout, adding a dynamic flow to the property. Just that half-height glimpse of the room upstairs through the glass panels gives a more organic, domestic feel to the layout of the lower living room area.

I divided the drawing room into two spaces. These spaces were reflected in the shape of the silk ivory carpets (each with an integral geometric pattern, handmade by Stark) that we put over the top of dark Versailles parquet floors – one decorated to a circular theme, the other to the remaining rectangular shape. Individually coffered ceilings also delineate the different spaces. The back section has a comfy, circular seating area which complements the curve of the lovely Steinway grand piano and invites you to 'gather round'. With no beautiful vistas through windows the focal point has to be central, hence making a virtue of the rounded seating arrangement and its circular-sectioned coffee table.

In the other, more linear section of the drawing room, I worked hard to establish two strong focal points. In such a large space, it is imperative to have visually engaging objects of interest to root you in the surroundings and prevent that feeling of floating away into a featureless, flat-walled space. Tim Gosling crafted a stunning, wall-hung cabinet which is suspended along one wall. At first glance it could be a large, shuttered window with a lovely panelled casement, but it is in fact a clever display cabinet which artistically frames (and happily loses to the burr walnut backdrop) the large TV screen that is essential today. The eye is drawn to the cleverly top-lit glass shelves on either side of the screen which showcases an alluring collection of Chinese sang-de-boeuf porcelain and other artefacts. Porcelain glazes often up pick up colours of surrounding items so the grouping projects a lively feel of its own. For the second focal point, I installed a wide floor-to-ceiling chimney breast of stunning book-matched statuary marble. You cannot beat the glow of a fire as a visual draw.

Tim and I worked hard to use 'light and dark' as a decorative theme, and to play with shapes (curves, octagons, rectangles) to bring softness and comfort into a harsh architectural shell. The client wanted custom-made pieces of furniture to suit the spaces. The wall-hung television cabinet on the far wall is fashioned from a serene pale-honey ripple sycamore with inlays of bronze and a rich, dark burr walnut

interior. In contrast, but in sympathy with the book-matched marble chimney breast, the twinned half-moon console tables on either side of the fireplace are made in dark stained walnut with tops inset with glass and bandings of nickel; these are topped with light cut-out nickel lamp bases and positioned beneath black-and-white self-portrait photographs by Tseng Kwong Chi, posed in front of iconic architectural facades in London and Rome. The octagonal tables on either side of the sofa complement the octagonal backs of the wood-framed armchairs. The low coffee table is sumptuous in size and made in Santos rosewood, again with bandings of nickel. The top glass sections are designed to float in planes; their display of fossils and ammonites make a good talking point. Putting prehistoric items in a contemporary environment gives them extra status, and the coils and spirals embellish our decorative play on shapes. For the soft furnishings, I decorated to a palette of ivory, silver, pale taupe and dusky pink, layering silk on velvet, smooth textiles on woven weaves, and so on.

Left: *I divided the long, rectangular drawing room into two living spaces reflected in the shape of the silk ivory carpets and the individually coffered ceilings.*
Below: *In a room without windows, this clever display cabinet which frames the large TV screen is a focal point. Top-lit glass display shelves showcase Chinese sang-de-boeuf porcelain.*

The striking painting by Nabil Nahas we acquired from Ben Brown perfectly encapsulates the rich, contemporary, organic theme of the room.

Glass doors throughout the ground floor maximise the light between the spaces. Each is outlined with a light art deco-esque bronze pattern to unify the decorative theme. At this level of luxury interior decoration, it is all about incredibly subtle, complementary details that add up to a design sympathy you 'feel', rather than a collection of A, B and C that knocks you out. Up the floating stairs from the drawing room, you come to the client's study, which rejoices in a pair of 'normal' windows. The desk faces these outlook windows, which I framed with sculptural straight pelmets in watered silk, adorned with intricate braiding motifs that echo the architectural detailing on the doors. This is the sitting area where men do business deals. The overall aim was for an ultra-sophisticated calmness; the polar opposite of visual busyness or ostentation. To achieve this, it is important to stick to a theme and not introduce too many different materials. The inbuilt joinery matches the walnut and ivory lacquer of the furniture. Again I have picked a neutral shade silk wool mix carpet, but lined and edged it with cream leather for textural interest. The deep buttoned chesterfield adds a jewel of colour to the room while the funky 1960s print on the stools adds a dash of levity in a masculine palette of plum, grey, black and taupe. The stage beyond hiding technology is to turn the disguise into a decorative work of interest in itself, so the audiovisual wall has been built to resemble a sleek chimney breast. On the walls, an intriguing metallic wall sculpture by Curtis Jere adds ornamental relief; there is also a gorgeous 3D canvas – again by Nabil Nahas – covered in starfish and layered with high-chroma gold acrylic paint, which lends beauty and an element of surprise.

Without doubt, the dining room was the dullest square shell of a room. I am always working to create something unique and special for clients, but here I had to come up with a truly whimsical, extravagant flight of fancy to make a feature of this prime entertaining room. The result is a dreamlike tropical rainforest wrought from ornamental plaster relief walls to create a spectacular interior landscape. Trees, bees, bullrushes, butterflies, peacocks, birds of paradise, fronds and ferns… The walls are an exotic jungle assembled from more than a hundred square metres of hand-applied plaster panels which are up to five centimetres in relief. I had experimented before with the potential of a richly ornamental plaster wall in a small space, so it was a dream come true to have free rein to implement it as a decorative backdrop here on such a lavish scale. It was a labour of love for the team from plaster specialists Hayles and Howe, and it looks completely fabulous. Every single tiny shape on the thirty-foot long walls was individually moulded in the

Left: *A warm fire blazing in the wide, floor-to-ceiling chimney breast in book-matched statuary marble consolidates the design play on 'light and dark'.*

Left: *How to enliven the dullest square of a dining room? A whimsical flight of fancy wrought in ornamental plaster relief creates a unique interior landscape in this prime entertaining space.* **Above:** *Tim Gosling designed the beautiful dining table so that it can be used as one big surface or as two more intimate settings.*

workshop and came wrapped in tissue paper, ready to be applied to pre-made panels. We opted not to paint it in multiple colours, but just to stipple the surface and finish off with a slightly glossy sheen to maximise the relief effect.

That was the backdrop, but to do the plasterwork justice, lighting was super critical. With Sanjit's innovative approach, we were determined to light it all softly so that the whole perimeter was lit. Light sources were installed from above and from below using underlit glass panels to replicate the feeling of daylight. The ceiling-recessed wall washers create an even light without forming harsh shadows, while the glass floor was backlit with concealed LED (light emitting diodes) strip lights to add an extra dimension to the end wall and complement the natural daylight filtering in from the skylight above. The ceiling was reconfigured to create one large coffer to add height with a further layer of light. I commissioned two fresh and delicate circular crystal chandeliers from Dominic Phillips; these frame the fireplace and work well above the beautiful table which Tim designed in two parts so it can be used as one big dining surface or two more intimate settings.

Further play on light and spaciousness was achieved through the furniture and decoration. I love the way Tim has cut the pedestals for the Chinoiserie urns with Perspex so that they appear to float. Each urn is slightly different in design, but they feed off each other incredibly well in the surreal floating formation. We arranged a variety of glass objects on top of the cabinets; these are of a different style, age and value and are

united only by the coral/rust/red palette. I adore the rich, warm vibrancy of red as an accent colour. The handmade rug picks out the organic chestnut or red-earth tint and the floral silk on the back of the wooden-back dining chairs evokes the frond, plant and forest motifs in the walls. We used plain, neutral silk fabric on the seats to keep it light and also to tie in with the tone of the plaster relief walls. In terms of visual dynamics, the faceted mirrored chimney breast above the wide fireplace and mantel is incredibly important. The reflection of the jungle features further envelops you in the lush surroundings. The positioning of a dramatic photograph by Candida Höfer, who celebrates vast empty space within stunning architectural surrounds, gives the room an amazing extra sense of perspective.

In contrast, the cinema-cum-media room does not rely on light as an embellishment; we simply up-lit the walls subtly to lift the space a bit and give the illusion of height. A subterranean feel only adds to the escapist comfort of curling up in front of a good movie. Here, the priority was to create intimacy. Wool fabric is stretched over panels and hung slightly off the wall to add warmth and depth. The space is lit softly to give an illusion of a higher ceiling and is decorated with iconic photographs of Hollywood greats. The most important furnishing element in a home cinema is supremely comfy seating. It is a one-function room and otherwise needs to be kept simple. A deep and capacious squidgy sofa hugs three sides of the walls so a few people can stretch out or a larger number can sit in comfort. I have added two La-Z-Boy recliners in smart navy blue

(they do everything for you; it is like flying first class) and a pair of versatile and pretty yin and yang stools, plus a pile of beanbags as seats for kids. A line-up of three simple cubes, made decorative with specialist, ripple-effect veneer, makes a smooth and functional drinks and popcorn station. The screen wall is kept sleek with inbuilt cupboards and drawers for the technology, handsets, film menus and computer games.

Upstairs, the master bedroom is very peaceful; an oasis of calm which benefits from natural light, courtesy of two generous windows. It is quite unusual in that you come into the bedroom at one level – the seating area – and go down two steps to the lower sleeping level; two sleek low bookcases, custom-made from peachy blonde sycamore, delineate the space. Sycamore

is used again, in combination with shagreen and ivory handles on the matching dressing table and bedside cabinets. The colour scheme of peachy blonde, duck-egg blue and coral emanates from the beautiful Rubelli woven silk used on the headboard. This room is a masterclass in silk. As a fabric, silk can take you through a gamut of textures, from the roughness of raw silk to the smoothest satin. The walls are upholstered in panels covered in the warm peachy blonde tone, and we have worked hard to match the linear panel boarding on the walls with the lines in the headboard. Likewise, the curves of the furniture edges are complemented by the scrolling on the wooden arms of the chairs.

Mining the rich seam of a specific palette means that every detail is considered. Take the silk curtains; they hang in

Left: *Soft perimeter lighting is critical to do the plasterwork justice. Ceiling-recessed wall washers create an even light while glass decorative objects and mirroring allow the rainforest to 'live' through the dining room furniture.*
Above: *The serene bedroom scheme extends through to the seating area where the swirling emerald tones in the painting 'Green Target' after Jasper Johns by Vik Muniz adds a zingy focal point to a space without windows. Note how the lighting - the uniformly lit coffer and concealed lighting with the cabinets - plays an important role in a tricky space with different ceiling heights and floor levels.*

- The impact of a hall is visually important but also in a practical sense for the preservation of sanity in a busy household. Keep the hall clean and tidy at all costs – even if the rest of the house is unbelievably messy.
- Coffered ceilings with lights installed around the rim of the recessed section, are an excellent way to counter low ceiling height.
- A pile of beanbags, which you can stow away when not required, makes good extra seating for kids.
- To achieve more depth of field on flat walls, hang art or photography which features perspective – as I did here with Candida Höfer's celebrations of vast empty space within stunning architectural surrounds.

generous tailored folds under a simple box pelmet, augmented by a slight contrast band – satin on silk – which is edged with a subtle waterfall of silk tassels. Superficially the curtains are one colour, but the sense of luxury comes from the different textures and shades. This extends to the sumptuous, pure silk, handmade carpet for the ultimate in barefoot comfort.

The seating area in the bedroom continues with the serene colour palette. However, an immensely strong, zingy element is added by the intense, swirling palette of jade, emerald and moss tones in the painting Green Target after Jasper Johns by Vik Muniz. The occasional tables, like the large square, glass coffee table, are supported by softly-woven, gold-leaf bases, bringing the room to life. As elsewhere, the lighting played an important role in a tricky space with different ceiling heights and floor levels. The uniformly-lit coffer and concealed lighting within the cabinets helps to tie the room together and makes full use of the space.

Right above: *A play of different light effects highlights the luxurious custom-made fittings in a bathroom.*
Right below: *Two steps framed by sleek, low bookcases delineate the seating from the sleeping area in the master bedroom.*
Far right: *The main bedroom is a masterclass in silk. Led by the sumptuous Rubelli weave on the headboard, silk in its various textural guises extends onto the wall panels, curtains, carpet and soft furnishings.*
Overleaf: *The most important element in a media-cum-cinema room is versatile and supremely comfy seating. Here, wool fabric panels hung slightly off the wall add warmth and intimacy. The space is lit softly to give an illusion of a higher ceiling and is decorated with iconic photographs of Hollywood greats.*

ST JAMES'S

Previous: *Like a majestic cathedral spire, this statement chandelier draws the eye upwards to the original glass skylight from the heart of the remodelled property. Its intricate beauty radiates not just gorgeous luminosity but also a sense of opulence and luxury.*
Far left: *The ceiling of the Marble Hall features an oval coffered panel painted to reflect a blue sky edged with wispy white cloud. The use of white adds oxygen to the palette of strong reds and greens which signal the richness of colour that will be explored throughout the ground floor.*
Below: *The space has the full armoury of classic vestibule features: marble columns, panelled walls trimmed with plenty of 22-carat gilding and a series of torchere wall sconces.*
Overleaf: *At the centre of the new frontage, a grand opulent entrance leads into a new Marble Hall and further into an Inner Hall. We had to aggrandise the traditional domestic greeting room to reflect the palatial size of the property.*

Whether working on a penthouse, a cottage or a large sprawling country house, my mantra is always to consider a design proposition in bite-sized chunks. Never have I had to heed my own advice more than when I was commissioned to create an opulent *hôtel particulier* from four adjoining Grade 1 listed terrace houses overlooking St James's Park, the oldest of the Royal Parks in London. The French coined the phrase *hôtel particulier* for the palatial mansions built by nobles for their official city residences and it beautifully evokes the sense of grandeur and prime location involved here.

The great joy of working in interior design is variety. No two jobs are the same. On each assignment you encounter new challenges, explore novel ideas and techniques according to your clients' individual ideas and the state of their property. This project – which is considered to be the second largest restoration project in London after St Pancras Station - was an immense and stimulating undertaking on every level, and a satisfying way to draw on 25 years of training and experience.

From initial site visit to the triumphant placing of the final cushion, it was a four-year process of intense collaborative effort. I worked with senior designers Mathew Claridge, Merideth Paige and Susie Beart – serious collective brainpower – and, between us, we assessed the existing historical content, fittings and layout of the four houses before embarking on the space planning and re-modelling necessary for them to work as one magnificent property. Once the framework was established, we continued our historical research and consultation to fine-tune the core decorative schemes. There was much to-ing and fro-ing with the client representatives, Kevin Martindale and Jane Wagner. We bonded as a team; friends for life.

How to describe the scale of the job? In purely numerical terms, the project encompassed the restoration and refurbishment of 94 rooms (including halls and lobbies), which included 16 bedrooms and 25 bathrooms or cloakrooms. The evolution of the interior called for 36 chandeliers, 27 lanterns, 2,662 metres of bespoke curtain lining and 372 bespoke cushions. For the 93 windows that required treatments, we commissioned 81 pairs of curtains, 56 pairs of sun curtains, 25 Roman blinds or Venetian shades and 90 roller blinds. We collated more than 187 presentation boards to the clients and placed 4,500 separate orders for items. The minutely detailed Decoration Schedule/Specification ran to 217 pages.

Left: *A Regency-style laylight pours light into the grandiose Inner Hall which sits at the heart of the newly configured property. The shape of the ceiling feature is repeated in the inlaid marble floor. Further light and perspective come from murals which celebrate landscape views of St James's Park.*
Below: *The potentially dark Inner Hall is beautifully lit to create a sense of spaciousness and serenity at the heart of the property.*

In terms of structural scale, the 'new' property comprised four white stucco-faced houses on the south side of the terraces overlooking St James's Park. They were built between 1827 and 1832 in accordance with the designs of John Nash, the architect responsible for much of the layout of Regency London (under the patronage of George IV, initially as Prince Regent then as King) as well as the Royal Pavilion in Brighton and large sections of Buckingham Palace. My client's Pall Mall houses had variously been grand homes to members of the Establishment and the ruling elite; former residents amount to a roll-call of names such as William Gladstone, the 3rd Earl Grey, General Robert Balfour, the Earl of Lonsdale and Lord Cowdray. Between the wars, one of the buildings had housed Crockford's Club, a raffish gentlemen's gambling establishment.

The job therefore required a vision of an elevated type of grandeur. The exterior of all the houses, and the 1867 Owen Jones interior of one (of which, more below), are Grade 1 listed, meaning they are buildings 'of exceptional interest' and their historic fabric is safeguarded by bodies such as English Heritage and the Crown Estate. A cornerstone of the brief was the creation of two new state reception rooms; a large salon and a small dining room. A state room, according to standard definition, is one of a suite of very august and lavishly decorated rooms designed to impress distinguished guests, a head of state, even a monarch. It is my belief that the two we were commissioned to fashion here are the first two state rooms to be created in a private house since the War.

One of the four houses rejoiced in a bold, Grade 1 listed interior designed by Owen Jones, who was one of the most influential design theorists of the 19th century. Jones was inspired by the Islamic world, with its traditional geometric patterned ornamentation and robust colour palette. The luxurious interiors he wrought in the 1860s, both inside the Nash envelope of this property and in the Cairo palace belonging to Isma'il Pasha, the Viceroy of Egypt, are lauded for his creative application of Arab and Moorish design principles. We found an extraordinary melange of decoration, veneers, panels, plasterwork, friezes and these fabulous, overwhelming ceilings. To analyse the original colours and authenticate our restoration plans to meet the approval of bodies such as English Heritage we had various historians and experts gently scraping off paint with palette knives, scientifically dating the pigments and so on.

The Owen Jones heritage was the design footprint that would lead our restoration scheme. Take the Library, for example, and its extraordinary, ornate, High Gothic ceiling [direct to picture detail]. It could almost be a colour plate of pattern analysis from Owen Jones's seminal design publication, *Grammar of Ornament*. When the historic fabric is so audacious, you have to respect it and meet it head on.

We washed, cleaned, polished and restored the original carved and hand-painted ceiling and took its accents of emerald green and scarlet red as inspiration for the room's colour scheme. Having found the book cabinet in an upstairs room, we restored it and brought it back for library use. Mathew Claridge came across the amazing Colza chandelier in pieces, muddy and dirty, in a back room. It was brilliant of him to recognise it. Fully restored, it has the value of a serious piece of art. Here, its light beautifully offsets the glorious wall panelling and gilding, and the incredible complexity of the inlays around the architraves.

A house with this kind of history gives a contemporary decorator a blueprint. We thought through the window treatments so that they complemented the ceiling both in the choice of colours and in the variety of shapes made by the fall of the curtain fabric and furbelows, the lines and silhouettes created by the trims; the look is aesthetically pleasing and absolutely authentic. The silk carpet is designed to lightly mirror the geometric patterns in the ceiling without distracting

Left: *We found the Library's amazing Colza chandelier in pieces in a back room. Fully restored, its light offsets the glorious wall panelling and gilding, and the complexity of the inlays around t he architraves.*
Above: *The ornate High Gothic ceiling could almost be a colour plate of pattern analysis from Owen Jones's seminal design publication, Grammar of Ornament. We washed, cleaned, polished and restored the original carved and hand-painted ceiling and took its accents of emerald green and scarlet red as inspiration for the room's colour scheme.*
Right: *The rich textures of the soft furnishings play on the relief and depth of the carved canopy overhead.*

from its glories. The rich textures of the soft furnishings play on the relief and depth of the carved canopy overhead. Even the simplicity of the gold-framed glass coffee table corresponds subtly to the gilded lines in the panelling. Our guiding principle here – as throughout the property - was absolute sympathy to the original design.

The overall plan for the new residence was to feature a series of state rooms - two state reception rooms, two state dining rooms, library, study, entrance and inner halls, and a pair of state bedrooms; the rest of the building was divided to designate apartments to suit the tastes and requirements of different members of my client's extended family.

At the centre of the new frontage created by the four former separate houses I wanted to create a suitably imposing entrance, which would lead into a new marble hall and further into an inner hall. One should never underestimate the potential impact of an entrance hall. I've written before about how strongly I believe a visitor's first impression on stepping inside a front door must be the visual quintessence of the overall look and feel of a house. Here, we clearly had to aggrandise the

traditional domestic greeting room to reflect the palatial size of the property and the lavish style of entertainment it might host. The tone had to be opulent, grand, and I particularly wanted to reflect the park-front location which is so steeped in the history of Regency London.

Step inside the Marble Hall and you get that sense of a luxurious passage from the world outdoors to indoor splendour. It looks as if it was an original part of the house, but we created it from scratch. The ceiling is uplifting - an oval coffered panel painted to reflect a blue sky edged with wispy white cloud. The details of birds in flight create vibrancy and movement overhead while the use of white on wall panels, coving and the fireplaces adds oxygen to the palette of strong reds and greens which signal the richness of colour that will be explored throughout the ground floor. The design motif here is an oval within a rectangle. This is replicated in the inlaid marble floor and on the sections of wall panelling as well as the ceiling. The space has the full armoury of classic vestibule features: marble columns, panelled walls trimmed with plenty of 22-carat gilding and a series of *torchere* wall sconces which reflect beautifully in the mirrors.

The Marble Hall's practical purpose, of course, is to lead into our Inner Hall which sits at the heart of the newly configured property. This was a room created across the original party line of two houses - a potentially dark internal zone - so to ensure spaciousness and serenity we installed a glorious circular Regency-style laylight (i.e. a glazed panel set flush to the ceiling to fake the feel of daylight with an artificial light source). Again, the shape of the ceiling feature is repeated in the stunning inlaid marble floor. Every aspect of this room pleases the eye: the floor, the ceiling, the intricate gilding details that distinguish the moulding and panelling. The elegance and lightness of the neo-classical Regency style also sits easily with a few individual touches: for example, the symbolic animal motifs on the beaten silver door panels allow the symbols of Hindu faith to sit comfortably with English idiom.

We brought further light and perspective to the Inner Hall by commissioning a series of painted murals from Lucinda Oakes specifically to celebrate the landscape views of St James's Park from the house as they would have appeared when the house was built. The property stands on the site left after the demolition in 1825 of Carlton House. This had

Far left: *The Large State Dining Room had originally been two rooms knocked through to create office space. Our role was to undertake restoration of the 50 per cent that boasts the authentic Owen Jones ceiling and decorative effects, and replicate it across the other half.*
Left: *Every detail is inspired by the colours and motifs in Jones's own documentation of Indian Ornament for the Great Exhibition of 1851 and 1855.*
Overleaf: *The pattern in our replicate half of the ceiling includes Yantris symbols, intertwining triangles, Paisley patterns and a Dharma wheel.*

been the residence of the Prince Regent and the stimulus for John Nash's creation of a ceremonial route from St James's to Regent's Park via Regent Street, Portland Place and Park Square. The redevelopment of the site prompted a scheme for the improvement of St. James's Park, which Nash then laid out in the manner of landscape designer Humphry Repton, breaking up the straight lines of the canal into the present lake with islands. Lucinda's murals and the *grisaille* panels over the door celebrate this heritage.

The Large State Dining Room, which seats 34 around one long table, had originally been two rooms knocked through to create one large space for Crown Estate offices. Our role was to undertake restoration of the fifty per cent that boasts the authentic Owen Jones ceiling and decorative effects, and replicate it across the other half. Rather than copying the original motifs, we introduced in the original palette of muted reds, browns, blues, greens and gilding some Indian Hindu

Below and right: *A house with this kind of history gives a contemporary decorator a blueprint. Inspired by the classic genre called 'Grotesque', we designed the ceiling pattern of the Small State Dining Room, below, and commissioned a silk carpet to reflect it on the floor.* **Overleaf:** *Note the intensely rich Regency-inspired drapery in this absolute jewel-box of a room. I wanted to bring in a beautiful royal blue offset by gold.*

symbols and motifs to reflect the culture of our client. Jones had documented Indian Ornament for the Great Exhibition of 1851 and 1855 so we could quite authentically include Yantris symbols (patterns of circles within squares, symbols of balance and focus), intertwining triangles (representing the balance of opposing forces), Paisley patterns and a Dharma wheel (representing duty).

The intensity of embellishment in the room is extraordinary – reds, greens, golds, stripes, motifs, geometric shapes, stylised floral shapes, you name it, the whole intoxicating High Gothic package. Underneath the dark green dado rail which runs around the room, we designed decorative panelling to incorporate motifs from the ceiling and the room. It looks like exquisite marquetry, but every detail was applied with paint. This was restoration of the most sensitive type.

We designed the furniture and had it made in England, France, Italy, and as far afield as India and China. This was not just because nothing suitable was available to buy from salesrooms; historically, in a house of this stature, furniture would have been designed for the space it was intended. Mathew also designed the carpet to reflect the ceiling and incorporate Hindu motifs. We sourced fabrics, wallpapers and *passementerie* from Watts of Westminster - an offshoot of the grand decorating house Watts & Co, which was founded by leading 19th-century architects to market textiles, embroideries and wallpapers. A room of this scale and exuberance needs serious chandeliers and we had these made and gilded in Italy.

The Small State Dining Room is a perfect cube that seats 14 around a gorgeous circular table with lapis lazuli inserts. The table – and matching credenza - was designed by David Linley and incorporates circular and semi-circular motifs to reflect the close relationship between the furniture and the architectural elements throughout the property. The dining chairs are made by Reed and Rackstraw, the fine English chair specialists who were also responsible for the chairs in the Large State Dining Room. On our first site visit, we had found two pairs of columns in random dark corners of the houses. When we first assessed this room as a shell, we saw that we could relocate the granite pair inside the entrance here. That was the starting point; and the room's appealing cube shape inspired the desire to create an absolute jewel-box of a room. Note the intensely rich Regency-inspired drapery. I wanted to bring in a beautiful royal blue offset by gold. There was no colour scheme with that depth of blue in the Owen Jones interior - and if you are going to be bold and create a state room, you are not going to go beige!

We did not want to copy or do a pastiche of a room. We wanted to design and be led by our own 'original' ceiling, inspired by the classic genre called 'Grotesque' after the extravagant form of Roman decorative art. This features ornamental arrangements of arabesques, garlands and small and fantastic human and animal figures set out in a symmetrical pattern around some form of architectural framework. The disciplines

Left: *An elevated type of grandeur: each glass element of the oversized chandelier which illuminates three floors of a grandiose stairwell was hand-blown according to Murano tradition by Il Vetro dei Dogi in Venice.*
Above: *The intricacy of the multicoloured glass adds luminosity and harmony with the original glass skylight above.*
Overleaf and pages 203-4: *A veritable fairy princess room: the Large State Reception Room boasts an extraordinary luminosity thanks to a concoction of the highest quality gold and crystal, shimmering silk and four knock-out chandeliers.*

of interior design I enjoy most are space planning and coming up with the design concepts for each room. I like to say I think in 3D and I knew exactly what I had in mind for the ceiling here. From that outline, we researched historical references and Mathew found an expert historical draughtsman to draw up the ceiling pattern.

The result is this beautiful painted ornamental square with a centre bed - part plaster, part paintwork – and motifs of camel (which symbolise wisdom in Hinduism), monkey (wit), elephant (strength) and bird (love). It took the team from Sterling Studios a few weeks up ladders painting on their backs in the manner of Michangelo to complete. The ornamental bed is framed by a gilt coving, then a cornice, a frieze and a further ornate frieze working away from the centre towards the point where the panelled walls meet the ceiling. We had parquet laid on the floor, topped by a silk carpet designed to reflect the ceiling, made in France by Atelier Pinton.

Historically, a glossy, light, bright interior was a sign of wealth and grandeur, intimidation and statement. Before electricity, people lived with bright colours and lots of mirrors and reflective gold. Rooms radiated with the clever use of reflected light. Just think of the effect gained by putting a single sconce with eight candles in front of a mirror: double the number of pools of light. We added engraved mirror panels of *verre églomisé*, a process in which the back of the glass is gilded with gold and designs are engraved – here with motifs taken from the Owen Jones template. All the gold in the room is 22-carat, and laid on leaf by leaf.

Nothing could be more romantic than the Large State Reception Room – a veritable fairy princess room. What thrills me about it is its extraordinary luminosity. The rectangular salon is furnished with a concoction of the highest quality gold and crystal, shimmering silk and four knock-out chandeliers, all wrought in extraordinary levels of decorative detail; but there is nothing oppressive about it. A first glimpse is like opening a door on a room with a thousand lit candles inside. I always find it exciting to watch people's faces when they are struck by its dramatic impact for the first time.

For me, this room was a once-in-a-lifetime opportunity to draw on 25 years of experience. We re-polished the other

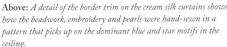

Above: *A detail of the border trim on the cream silk curtains shows how the beadwork, embroidery and pearls were hand-sewn in a pattern that picks up on the dominant blue and star motifs in the ceiling.*
Opposite: *The Private Study features modern furnishings inside the classic interior led by another jewel of an Owen Jones ceiling.*
Overleaf: *The colour palette of the furnishings in the original L-shaped Drawing Room is inspired by the gloriously multi-coloured Owen Jones enamel mantelpieces and ornate ceiling.*

pair of rescued original columns - two green marble ones – and used them to frame the double mahogany doors and set the tone of grandeur in a room that can accommodate up to 120 people standing with a glass of champagne. The discipline of the colours here is notable – perhaps 80 different colours all on the quiet palette. The ceiling is an intricate and delicate design painted in exquisite detail over months by the Sterling Studios team. We hung four Cinderella-at-the-ball chandeliers, which were wrought from glass hand blown by master craftsmen at Il Viettro di Doge in Venice, as were the glass and gilt wall lights and the light stands. The chandeliers arrived in London in thousands and thousands of pieces and it took three men a week to assemble them before the hanging process. Even the Louis XV furniture - in white and gilt with inlaid marble tops, commissioned and made in Paris – adds an element of shimmery lightness. The silk carpet echoes the ceiling with an added Savonnerie influence and was made by Atelier Pinton. When you reel off an inventory of the room, it sounds 'heavy', but it's all about achieving the right balance in an appropriate setting.

We created the state bedrooms – which we termed the Blue State Bedroom and the Red and Gold State Bedroom – in the idiom of the historical context. Designed to complement the proportion of the rooms and the very grand architecture, they needed to be of a luxuriousness suitable for important guests and family members but also designed with the modern practical requirements such as power showers and dressing-rooms in mind. The client wanted a masculine and a feminine bedroom, hence the differing colour schemes of Empire red and gold bolstered by highly polished mahogany, and silky powder blue softened by gilt and white furniture.

A state bedroom is a room you can spend the whole day in, a boudoir, a cocoon of luxury with a sumptuous half-tester bed, a dressing table for 'hair and make up', a breakfast/dining table, comfortable seating arrangement to receive visitors and an adjoining bathroom and dressing room. In a bedroom, I always start with the core colour and then add in my coordinates. The bigger a room, the more layers and interest you can add. The fabrics here are the absolute best embroideries, silks and bespoke finishes; all the *passementerie* was custom-designed to match

the fabrics. The detail in the process and quality control was intricate – right down to approval of individual threads.

In contrast to the state reception rooms, the original Drawing Room is on the first floor. A huge L-shaped room, it is notable for its grand proportions and two extraordinary Owen Jones enamel mantelpieces, the like of which I have never seen before. The chandeliers originate from the house's gambling era. We had them taken down, disassembled, cleaned and polished piece by piece so that they certainly sparkle now. Again, the ceiling is gloriously multi-coloured and rich in pattern and relief. Conscious of the size of the room, and the enormous amount of furnishing and upholstery it would demand, I was quickly up a ladder to pick out the full range of colours in the ceiling that we could echo below. I found golds, blues, greens and, surprisingly, a peachy pink tone. From that palette, we worked on layering colour, pattern and trims on sofas, cushions, Ottomans, side chairs, armchairs, curtains, stools, skirted side tables and the conversation piece. The space needed a lot of stature in terms of colour and interest to prevent it being dwarfed by the ceiling. A huge percentage of the 372 bespoke cushions we had made for this job can be found here!

Fittingly for a room that will doubtless entertain distinguished guests from overseas, we drew upon a truly international mix of luxury fabric houses: Fortuni and Rubelli from Italy; Burgin, Chanee Ducrocq, Lelievre and Edmund Petit from France; Watts and the Gainsborough Silk Weaving Company from the United Kingdom; and Janel Yonaty of the United States for exquisite trimmings. All the furniture is bespoke, from China, while the marquetry and woodwork is British. We had hundreds of distinguished craftsmen and artists involved in this one room, including the couturier and interior decorator Tomasz Starzewski whose embroiderers created the beautiful panels around the silk velvet Ottoman and various cushions. A team of couturiers from Jon Rhodes made possibly the most beautiful curtains ever seen – layer upon layer of silk and trim and damask and tassel and velvet. The walls are covered with woven silk panels from Lelievre.

As well as the genuinely decorative elements, we also worked in an air-conditioning system. The china display

Far left: *Talk about 'eye candy': the L-shaped Drawing Room is notable for its grand proportions and extraordinarily beautiful Owen Jones enamel mantelpieces.*
Left above: *The space demanded an enormous amount of colour and interest to prevent it being dwarfed by the overhead decoration.*
Left below: *Hundreds of distinguished craftsmen and artists contributed to the Drawing Room, including the couturier and interior decorator Tomasz Starzewski whose embroiderers created the beautiful panels around this silk velvet Ottoman.*
Overleaf: *I went up a ladder to pick out the full range of colours in the intricate ceiling that we could echo below and found golds, blues, greens and, surprisingly, a peachy pink tone.*

cabinet, the design of which is copied from an antique piece, was made with a false back to house the air-con mechanics yet still leave enough space to display a selection of pretty ornamental plates.

In addition to the state rooms, I am particularly fond of the private study we designed for our client. It sits in the corner of the first floor, behind the Drawing Room in the original Owen Jones house, and thus boasts another jewel of a ceiling, which again was the starting point for our design. Here though, with so many formal and grand rooms already, we chose to continue to 'play the game' but with modern furnishings inside the classical interior. We took the blue in the star formations in the ceiling and covered the walls down to the dado rail in an intense cerulean silk satin so luxurious you want a ball dress in the same fabric. This incredible blue sits above satinwood inlaid marquetry panelling which matches the original Owen Jones mirror and chimney piece.

Into this classic shell, we hung exquisite cream wool and silk curtains which are distinguished by a generous border trim of beadwork, embroidery and hand-sewn pearls, worked in a pattern that picks up on the Owen Jones motifs. The contemporary cream-on-cream carpet also contains in its surface pattern an echo of the ceiling geometry. We commissioned a desk from Italy, a television cabinet custom-made in walnut, a pair of console tables from Tim Gosling and square-backed chairs upholstered in a funky blue geometric pattern from David Linley. The fabulous 1930s-style white leather chairs with red velvet back and seat panels add panache. All the team love this room – a cameo, I feel, of my philosophy of combining the contemporary with the traditional in a visually exciting way.

Left: *The luxuriousness of the Red and Gold State Bedroom is bolstered by a sumptuous half-tester bed, highly polished mahogany furniture and gold finishes.*
Right, above and below: *An example of a gentlemen's and a ladies' cloakroom. The four-year restoration project encompassed the refurbishment of 94 rooms, which included 25 bathrooms or cloakrooms.*
Overleaf: *The fabrics in the Blue State Bedroom are the absolute best embroideries, silks and bespoke finishes; all the passementerie was custom-designed to match the fabrics and the detail in the process and quality control was intricate, right down to the approval of individual threads.*

TIPS
- Whatever the scale of your redecoration project, divide your plan into bite-size chunks to keep focused and relaxed.
- Listen to the architecture of your home and pay homage to it.
- Colour. If your starting point is bold historic fabric, make sure to meet it head on.

GLOSSARY

Arts & Crafts – an aesthetic movement from the latter half of nineteenth-century England, led by William Morris. The movement stood for traditional craftsmanship, using simple forms and often employed medieval, romantic or folk styles of decoration.

Bonhams – a privately owned British auction house and one of the world's oldest and largest auctioneers of fine art and antiques. The Bonhams name is recognised worldwide, throughout all sectors of the fine arts, antiques and collectors markets.

Chaise longue – an upholstered, high backed chair, seat or armchair with an extended seat area that is long enough to support the legs, allowing a person to recline.

Chinoiserie – a European style of decoration, derived from Chinese traditional design in late eighteenth-century France and England. It is characterised by its use of occasionally fanciful imagery of an imaginary China and employment of lacquer-like materials and decoration.

Christie's – currently the world's largest art business and a fine arts auction house. Its main headquarters are in St. James's, London, where it has been based since 1823, and Rockefeller Plaza, New York.

Commode – an elaborate French form of chest of drawers, often highly decorated and extremely popular throughout Europe in the eighteenth century. It would traditionally be a piece of veneered case furniture, much wider than it was high, containing drawers or shelves, usually concealed behind doors, extending the full width of the front and with a marble slab top.

Corian – the brand name for a solid surface material created by DuPont scientists in 1967. An original material of this type, it is composed of acrylic polymer and alumina trihydrate (ATH), a material derived from bauxite ore. Its primary use is as a countertop surface, although it has many other applications.

Coronet – a small crown consisting of ornaments fixed on a metal ring. By one definition, a coronet differs from a crown in that a coronet never has arches, and from a tiara in that it completely encircles the head.

Crown Estate – a property portfolio owned by the Crown, one of the largest property owners in the United Kingdom. Formally accountable to Parliament, the Crown Estate is managed by an independent organisation headed by the Crown Estate Commissioners. The surplus revenue from the Estate is paid each year to HM Treasury.

Eau de Nil – late nineteenth century: from French eau-de-Nil, literally 'water of the Nile'.

Elizabethan – an English design period corresponding to the reign of Queen Elizabeth I (1558-1603), often considered to be the golden age in English history. It was the height of the English Renaissance and saw the flowering of English poetry, music, literature and architecture. The Renaissance era manifested itself in large, square and tall houses, often with asymmetrical towers, hinting at the evolution from medieval fortified architecture.

English Heritage – an executive, non-departmental public body of the British Government sponsored by the Department for Culture, Media and Sport (DCMS). By advising on the care of the historic environment of England, English Heritage complements the work of Natural England, which aims to protect the natural environment.

Georgian – a style of architecture and decoration associated with the 'four Georges of England': George I, II, III and IV (1714-1810). It does not compromise a coherent entity, but combines Renaissance, Rococo and neo-classical elements, with predominantly classical forms. The first phase is dominated by a revival of Palladianism, manifested in furniture by the placing of classical pediments on cabinets. The late Italian Baroque style was copied as fervently as the French secretaires.

Gothic Revival – a revival of Gothic architecture that took place, largely in England, in the late eighteenth and early nineteenth centuries and was originally used in a spirit of playfulness and even mockery. From the beginning of the nineteenth century, the Gothic Revival began to be taken more seriously, and was applied to all types of public, private and ecclesiastical buildings, with features including decorative patterns, finials, scalloping and lancet windows.

Grisaille – a term for painting executed entirely in monochrome or near-monochrome, usually in shades of grey. It is particularly used in large decorative schemes, often to imitate marble relief. Grisaille paintings resemble the drawings, normally in monochrome, that artists of the Renaissance were trained to produce; like drawings, they can also betray the hand of a less talented assistant more easily than a fully coloured painting.

Jacobean – a style of architecture and decoration prevalent in England during the reign of

James I (1603-25). It combines Renaissance, Gothic and Palladian architectural motifs with strapwork and other decorative forms associated with Mannerism in northern Europe. The woodcarving, chiefly in dark brown oak, is highly elaborate and its furniture is somewhat heavy and complex.

Marquetry – an elaborate surface decoration using inlays in wood veneering. The pieces of veneer are of simple repeating geometric shapes, forming tiling patterns covering a floor or furniture. The veneers used are primarily woods, but may include bone, ivory, turtle-shell, mother-of-pearl, pewter, brass or fine metals. The simplest kind of marquetry uses only two sheets of veneer, which are temporarily glued together and cut with a fine saw, producing two contrasting panels of identical design.

Ormolu – an eighteenth century English term derived from the French for ground gold. It refers to gilded bronze or brass furniture mounts. Craftsmen principally used ormolu for the decorative mountings of furniture, clocks, lighting devices and porcelain; attaining their highest artistic and technical development in France. The ormolu technique was extensively used in French Empire mantel clocks, reaching its peak during this period.

Strapwork – a stylised representation in ornament of leather straps, consisting of flattened strips or bands of curling leather, parchment or metal cut into elaborate shapes, with piercings, and often interwoven in a geometric pattern. It became popular in England in the late sixteenth and seventeenth centuries as a form of decorative plasterwork moulding, used particularly on ceilings, but was also sculpted in stone, for example around doorways.

Palladianism – a style of architecture inspired by the works and publications of the sixteenth century Venetian architect Andrea Palladio. Brought to England in the seventeenth century by Inigo Jones, the style flourished in the eighteenth century.

Parquet – a geometric mosaic of wood pieces used for decorative effect. The two main uses of parquetry are patterns on furniture and block patterns for flooring. Parquet patterns are entirely geometrical and angular; the most popular parquet flooring pattern is herringbone. Timber contrasting in colour and grain are sometimes employed.

Passementerie – the art of making elaborate trimmings or edgings of applied braid, gold or silver cord, embroidery, beads, etcetera in various forms. Styles of passementerie include tassels, fringes (applied, as opposed to integral), ornamental cords, galloons, pompons, rosettes and gimps.

Pleach – the art form of tree shaping. Pleaching or plashing describes the weaving of branches into houses, furniture as veneer, ladders and many other three-dimensional art forms. Pleaching was commonly used in gardens from late medieval times to the early eighteenth-century, to create shaded paths or to create a living fence out of trees or shrubs.

Pugin – Augustus Welby Northmore Pugin (1 March 1812 – 14 September 1852) was an English architect, designer, artist and critic, chiefly remembered for his pioneering role in the Gothic Revival style; his work culminated in the interior design of the Palace of Westminster.

Rattan – palm bark used in thin strips for caning, weaving baskets and making furniture. Rattan accepts paints and stains and can be worked into many styles. Moreover, the inner core can be separated and worked into wicker.

Regency – a period in English architecture and design of the early nineteenth century, corresponding in date to the regency of Prince George, before he became George IV (1811-20). A version of neo-classicalism based on Greek rather than Roman prototypes; it also accommodates Egyptian, Chinoiserie and Rococo influences.

Sang-de-boeuf – an innovative glaze created using a reduction of copper and iron oxides at high temperature, meaning 'ox blood' in French. A difficult technique, first developed in China in the 13th century, it was reinvented by several art potters in Europe during the late nineteenth century.

Shagreen – a type of rawhide consisting of rough untanned skin, formerly made from a horse's back or that of an onager (wild ass). With an unusually rough and granular surface, Shagreen is now commonly made of the skins of sharks and rays and is sometimes used as a fancy leather for book bindings, pocketbooks and small cases, as well as its more utilitarian uses in the hilts and scabbards of swords and daggers, where slipperiness is a disadvantage.

Sir John Soane – an English architect who specialised in the Neo-Classical style. The son of a bricklayer, he rose to the top of his profession, becoming professor of architecture at the

Royal Academy and an official architect to the Office of Works, receiving a knighthood in 1831. His architectural works are distinguished by their clean lines, massing of simple forms, decisive detailing, careful proportions and skilful use of light sources.

Sisal – a species of agave with large fleshy leaves, native to southern Mexico but widely cultivated and naturalised in many other countries. Yielding a stiff fibre traditionally used for making rope and twine, it is also employed in many other things, such as paper, cloth, wall coverings, matting and dartboards.

Secretaire – a writing desk made up of two parts placed one above the other, the upper section with a hinged writing surface and the lower section with doors. One was often incorporated into a chest of drawers or bookcase in the eighteenth century and, from the second half of the century, various popular versions existed.

Sotheby's – one of the world's largest brokers of fine and decorative art, jewellery, real estate and collectibles. Sotheby's is the world's fourth oldest auction house in continuous operation, with ninety locations in forty countries. Originally British, it is now a multinational corporation headquartered in New York City.

Toile de Jouy – a French printed scenic cloth, consisting of a distinctive white or off-white background on which a repeated pattern of a single colour (most often black, dark red or blue) depicts a fairly complex narrative scene. Produced using rolled, engraved copper plates and first made in 1760 at Jouy en Josas.

Torchère – a candle or lamp with a tall stand of wood or metal. Originally, torchères were candelabra, usually with two or three lights. When first introduced in France towards the end of the seventeenth century, the torchère mounted one candle only, and when the number was doubled or tripled the improvement was regarded almost as a revolution in the lighting of large rooms.

Veneer – thin slices of wood, usually thinner than 3 mm, that are typically glued onto core panels to produce doors, parquet floors and parts of furniture. Veneer is obtained either by 'peeling' the trunk of a tree or by slicing large rectangular blocks of wood known as flitches. The appearance of the grain and figure in wood comes from slicing through the growth rings of a tree and depends upon the angle at which the wood is sliced.

Victorian – the design period in England and America corresponding to the reign of Queen Victoria (1837-1901). It often included interpretations and eclectic revivals of historic styles mixed with Middle Eastern and Asian influences. The name reflects the British and French custom of naming architectural styles after the reigning monarch.

Wilton – a carpet produced on a specific type of weaving machine called a wire loom. Wilton carpets are pile carpets whereby the pile is formed by inserting steel rods in the pile warps of the fabric. After the extraction of the rods, the pile is looped (if straight wires were used) or cut (if cutting wires were used). Wilton carpet is generally considered as high quality and is used for heavy-duty applications.

ACKNOWLEDGEMENTS

My first book, *Interiors for Living*, has been an interesting and stimulating experience – one that I could not have done alone. There are so many people to thank and I have made efforts with the list below. A very special thanks must be given to the kind clients who have permitted their marvellous houses to be featured in these pages, also to all my team members whose wonderful contributions have enabled me to create this book.

With my everlasting gratitude and in no particular order:

Kathanne Fowler
The Hinduja family
Kash Chandarana
Dr. Christopher Kelly and Shawn Donnelley
Lorraine Spencer
Jens Jakobsen
Caroline Brown
Stephen Woodhams
Jane Wagner
Mathew Claridge
Victoria Cooper
Merideth Paige
Susie Beart
Joan Somerville
Lucy Cox
Corbie Phillips
Mark van Oss
Andrew Buchanan
Stephen Lewis
Peter Greene
Sammy Lee
John and Dominic Phillips
The Team at Joanna Trading and Joanna Wood

Special thanks to all the brilliant contractors and craftsmen who have helped to achieve such stunning finishes.

To Sarah Edworthy for her encouragement, enthusiasm and ability to put my designer's vision into eloquent words on the page.

Last but never least, my husband Charles

IMPRINT

© Prestel Verlag, Munich · London · New York, 2014.
© for the text, Joanna Wood and Sarah Edworthy, 2014.

Prestel Verlag, Munich
A member of Verlagsgruppe Random House GmbH

Prestel Verlag
Neumarkter Strasse 28
81673 Munich
Tel. +49 (0)89 4136-0
Fax +49 (0)89 4136-2335

www.prestel.de

Prestel Publishing Ltd.
14–17 Wells Street
London W1T 3PD
Tel. +44 (0)20 7323 5004
Fax +44 (0)20 7323 0271

Prestel Publishing
900 Broadway, Suite 603
New York, NY 10003
Tel. +1 (212) 995-2720
Fax +1 (212) 995-2733

www.prestel.com

Library of Congress Control Number is available. British Library Cataloguing-in-Publication Data: a catalogue record for this book is available from the British Library; Deutsche Nationalbibliothek holds a record of this publication in the Deutsche Nationalbibliografie; detailed bibliographical data can be found under: http://dnb.d-nb.de

Prestel books are available worldwide. Please contact your nearest bookseller or one of the above addresses for information concerning your local distributor.

Editorial direction: Lincoln Dexter
Design and layout: Joana Niemeyer, April, London
Production: Friederike Schirge
Origination: Repro Ludwig, Zell am See
Printing and binding: Firmengruppe Appl, Wemding
Printed in Germany

ISBN 978-3-7913-4737-0

Endpapers: Jasper Peony Cirrus wallpaper by Lewis & Wood.

Picture Credits
© Tim Beddow, pages 8-25 and 180-216.
© Peter Bennett, pages 2-3, 6 and 102-141.
© Darren Chung, pages 162-179.
© Brent Darby, pages 82-101.
© photography Heiner Orth, production Sabine Wesemann, pages 4 and 26-81.
© Bruce Thomas, pages 142-161.

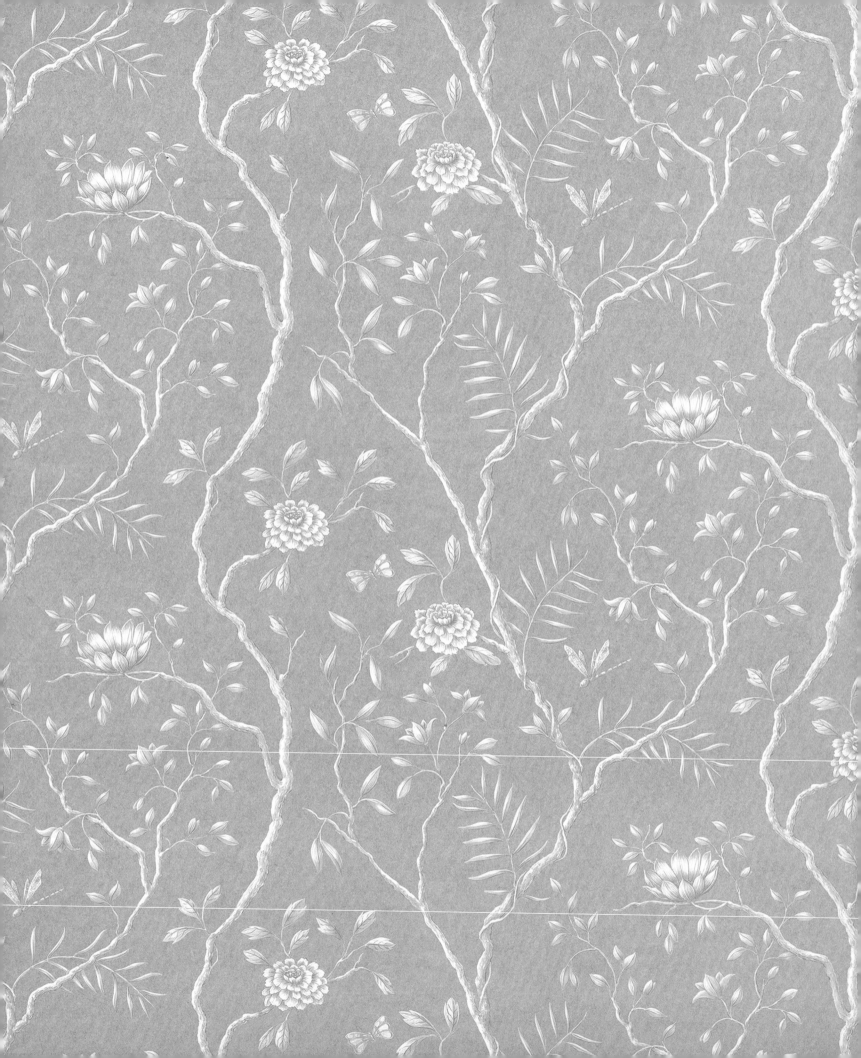